Quality assurance for social care agencies

A practical guide

Quality assurance for social care agencies

A practical guide

By
Emlyn Cassam and Himu Gupta

Published by Longman Industry and Public Service Management, Longman Group UK Ltd, 6th Floor, Westgate House, The High, Harlow, Essex CM20 1YR
Telephone Harlow (0279) 442601; Fax: Harlow (0279) 444501; Telex: 81491 Padlog

First published in 1992
Second impression 1993

A catalogue record for this book is available from the British Library.

ISBN 0-582-08944-1

Typesetting by: Typestyles (London) Limited, Harlow, Essex
Printed in Malaysia by PA

Contents

Acknowledgements		vii
Foreword		viii
1.	Introduction	1
	Checklist of main points	5
2.	From little acorns	6
	Checklist of main points	12
3.	What is this thing, quality assurance?	13
	Checklist of main points	20
4.	Creating the right climate	21
	Enthusiasm	22
	Imagination	27
	Maximisation	28
	Consultation	30
	Pride	32
	Checklist of main points	34
5.	Aims and values	35
	Aims and values of the organisation or agency	35
	Aims and values of the department	36
	Aims and values of the sections in the department	39
	Aims and values of individual units	40
	Caveat	40
	Advantages	42
	Checklist of main points	43
6.	Setting the standards	44
	Consumer care standards	48
	Standards for operational outputs	49
	Standards of inputs and processes necessary to achieve operational outcomes	51
	Checklist of main points	56

7. Setting up the assembly line 57
Instruction and direction 58
Training/staff development 60
Time, space and equipment 63
Checklist of main points 68

8. Monitoring and inspection 69
Monitoring 70
Inspection 73
The role of inspection units 79
Registration of private and voluntary residential homes 81
Checklist of main points 85

9. Consumer satisfaction 86
Designing the service 89
Setting standards and inspecting them 92
Service delivery 93
Informing the service user 94
After care services 95
Empowerment 96
Checklist of main points 98

10. Review of the system 99
Review of the departmental climate 99
Review of aims and values 100
Review of standards 101
Review of monitoring and inspection 102
Review of the whole system of quality assurance 103
Checklist of main points 104

11. Postscript 105

Appendix 1: Mission statement — Wiltshire County Council 108

Appendix 2: If you need to complain... We need to listen — Norfolk Social Services 112

Appendix 3: Statements of philosophy and policy for the provision of services — Norfolk Social Services 117

Acknowledgements

First and foremost, our appreciation must go to the Councillors and staff of Norfolk County Council, without whose vision and dedication much of this country's thinking about quality assurance would have been diminished. Our thanks too to David Wright, Norfolk's Director of Social Services, for his permission to quote from the Department's documents.

Our admiration goes to Clive Bone for his clear thoughts and his encouragement.

Our thanks to Anne Parker, CBE and Hugh Dunnachie of the Royal County of Berkshire, some of whose thinking we have unashamedly incorporated in this book.

Foreword

The past two decades have seen significant changes for the better in the management of quality within the UK, with continuous improvement throughout the period.

A little over 20 years ago, we had no national standards for quality systems and the responsibility for assuring the quality of products and services lay, to an undesirable extent, with the customer. Today, we have the situation where a very large number of companies and organisations of all kinds, in both the private and public sector, have introduced, or are introducing, quality systems which conform with national and international standards (BS5750/IS9000). Indeed, UK achievements in the assessment and certification, with national registration, of such companies and organisations, are probably unequalled anywhere else in the world. Quality assurance is now seen as a partnership between supplier and customer, with much greater reliance being placed on the suppliers for assuring the quality of their products and services.

This demonstrable improvement in UK quality managment did not occur spontaneously, however, it is the result of a great deal of dedicated and planned work and promotional effort by a considerable number of organisations and a great many people, from Government as the principal promoter, to the companies and organisations which introduced the quality systems. Principal contributors also include BSI, Certification Bodies, Local Authorities, NACCB, Professional Institutions, Universities and Colleges, Public Purchasing Authorities, Quality Consultants, Trade Associations and The British Quality Association (BQA) which has, as a principal objective, the promotion of best practices in quality management throughout the UK. The BQA's promotional role is executed largely through its Sector Quality Committees which, significantly, operate not only for the various industrial and commercial sectors, but also currently for Education and Training, Local Authorities and Social Care Agencies, the Sector Quality Committee for this last sector, having been chaired since its formation, by the co-author of this book, Mr Himu Gupta.

Much has been achieved but much improvement in UK quality management is still yet possible and necessary. The BQA and other organisations have therefore for several years now additionally been promoting Total Quality Management (TQM); this being a corporate management philosophy in which the accomplishment of quality is achieved by the personal involvement and accountability of all employees in an organisation, devoted to a continuous improvement process and committed to meeting customer needs.

As in TQM, quality promotion is aimed at a continuous improvement process and the authors of this book have made a welcome contribution to quality promotion in the important field of Social Care Agencies.

Bob Lonsdale CBE
Immediate past Chairman
BQA Board of Management

1 Introduction

The aims of this book are to be practical, readable and useful. Students who wish to delve into the arcana of theoretical concepts would be better advised to search elsewhere. During the last 5 years, the authors have devised and introduced a system of quality assurance into one of the largest social services departments in the country. Here, they describe how they did it, setting out the pitfalls and rewards, the successes and surprises.

The book will be of interest to anyone who is thinking of promoting the concepts of quality either in large organisations or in smaller teams and units. The impetus towards producing a quality outcome may be generated by councillors, managers, staff, consumers, voluntary bodies, professional associations, trade unions. All may benefit from reading this practical description of what works and what does not.

Of course, no one ever admits to having no interest in quality. Everybody would say that they intend to provide a good quality service, and are often affronted when obvious failures are starkly brought to their attention — often accompanied by hurtful publicity. Councils whose youngsters complain about intolerant or irrelevant regimes in their children's homes; proprietors of residential homes whose insensitivity denies dignity to their residents; staff whose restrictive practices force consumers into lifestyles even less flexible than penal institutions; voluntary organisation who so patronise their recipients that they have fewer rights than children; workers whose arrogance precludes their listening to what their clients are saying; politicians who promise Valhalla and deliver purgatory; all would probably claim that they are aiming at quality and 'doing the best they can'. And when things do go wrong, always the fault lies with 'resources' or incompetent bureaucrats or the profit motive or the Government or training — always something beyond their control. This book insists that quality must be the responsibility of everyone, and sets out what *you* can do to achieve it.

Aiming for quality in the work of social care agencies is not new. Achieving it, however, is somewhat rare. Practical instructions on how to tackle the task are few and uncoordinated. Like the pot of gold at the end of the rainbow, we all cherish the ambition of reaching it, but the precise route is difficult to find. Exhortations abound and there is no shortage of

Government strictures placing the full responsibility on local authorities for securing good standards of care.

> In managing the mixed economy of care, ensuring quality will be vital. No agency has a monopoly of virtue on quality. So far as local authorities are concerned the recent SSI report on the management of local authority homes for the elderly made that abundantly clear. We look to you to ensure that the care provided is not simply the cheapest, nor the most convenient to supply, nor a ratification of the way things have always been done, but the package that best meets the client's need. To define good quality is not always easy but I urge you to begin listening to your clients.
>
> David Mellor, Minister of Health,
> Social Services Conference 1989

> Monitoring the quality of services will become more complex as social services authorities' responsibilities for arranging the provision of community care increase. As purchasers, arrangers and providers of care services, local authorities must be responsible for ensuring that adequate systems are in place for securing the necessary qualit of services and monitoring it over time.
>
> Paragraph 5.14 of the White Paper
> *Caring for People*

> SSDs will need to ensure that they are aware of the quality of services which service users expect. This information can be obtained in a variety of ways but monitoring existing users' satisfaction with services, information obtained through the complaints procedure, from inspection units and from individual assessments, should be used. SSDs will be responsible for ensuring quality standards are built in to service specifications. A critical issue in commissioning care services will be the establishment of quality standards which meet the requirements of the 'purchaser', the service user and to which the service provider is committed. However, this does not mean that quality is solely the commissioner's responsibility. Providers are responsible for the delivery of quality and the onus should be placed on them to demonstrate the quality standards they propose and the systems in place to assure this provision.
>
> Paragraph 4.18 of Policy Guidance
> *Community Care in the Next Decade and Beyond*

In addition to these exhortations, experience from commercial and manufacturing ventures shows that concentration on quality not only leads to satisfied customers but increases the job satisfaction of the workers and reduces costs to the employer.

The Government too seems to be taking its own strictures seriously. Whatever people may think about the content of the *Citizen's Charter* and the *Patient's Charter*, or the rights of parents *vis-à-vis* their children's education, the concept is surely right. It is pleasing to see that (albeit slowly), the Government is taking steps to make some of the services over which it has more control more responsive to users e.g. Social Security and the Prison Service.

What then has been inhibiting social care agencies from putting quality 'up front'?

Disregarding the basic lack of understanding (which this book seeks to address), the prime reason is that some of the people vital to a comprehensive quality service have other issues higher on their agenda. Aiming for quality is fine, providing it does not get in the way of:

- some local and national politicians being able to keep down the costs to the charge payer or taxpayer;
- management stretching resources to meet preferred client need, or at least concentrating as a priority on those areas where there is the greatest danger of debilitating publicity. (And we have enough problems without upsetting the unions, don't we?);
- professionals, whose perceived task is to give people what they appear to need rather than what they would actually choose;
- those trade union negotiators who have no doubt where their loyalties lie when a choice has to be made between allocating extra money to benefit their members or to improve the standard of services.

Another inhibiting factor is the fear of losing control over what we want to do, the pernicious belief that we always know better than anyone else. Why should we have to do what somebody else wants, especially as we do not trust their values? What can the private sector (who have only been lured into social care by the prospect of making money) teach local authorities brought up on decades of municipal benevolence and public-spirited professionalism? Or, what lessons can protected town hall bureaucrats give to dynamic business entrepreneurs? What can either offer to dedicated, underfunded voluntary groups?

Even within departments or agencies suspicions have to be overcome. What are the hidden agenda? Is quality assurance merely a management device to discipline and control staff? Will it be used without consultation to change current ways of working? Why should staff co-operate if the end-results may reflect badly on them? What guarantees are there that deficiencies in personnel and training will be identified and rectified — or even the inefficiences of management? Where does it fit in with our equal opportunities policy? Will it just be an additional burden, an extra chore? What will it mean for *me*?

And councillors too may be wary. Why should they approve a system which will identify unmet need and consumer dissatisfaction? Is this a ploy by the officers to bounce the council into spending more money? What will the group make of it — and the chairs of other Committees?

Amongst these doubts and worries the voice of the consumer can be lost.

To overcome the inertia of the status quo and the fears of those deeply entrenched in their defensive postures is a complex and lengthy task. There is no quick fix. The introduction of a quality assurance system in Norfolk's Social Services Department was slow, evolutionary and painstaking — no big bang, no conversions on the road to Damascus — just an emerging vision which developed over 8 years. Many false trails were enthusiastically followed, including the chimera that inspection units on their own could raise standards; we found out in the very early days that merely to identify deficiencies did not necessarily mean that anything would be done about them!

Indeed, we are indebted to Clive Bone (of Clive Bone Associates) who recently pointed out to us that our experience was similar to that of Admiral Rickover who was in charge of the American nuclear submarine programme. We quote: 'Admiral Rickover was working in an environment that had first-class inspection facilities and comprehensive standards; yet in a 1962 Conference Paper 'The Never Ending Challenge' he wrote that:

- only 10% of the work was delivered to programme;
- 30% of the work was 6 months to a year late;
- 50% required rework on receipt;
- only 10% of the welds met the standard.'

This was happening in the most technically advanced nation on Earth, the nation that invented modern production engineering as it is understood today, and the nation that taught the Japanese about quality! In other words, Admiral Rickover was confronted with the inherent limitations of the control approach to quality. He saw that it was vital to ensure that the organisation which was to supply a product or service had a system of internal organisation to make sure that things were done right first time. Quality control — standards setting and monitoring — does not achieve this and can lead to too many controls and bureaucracy, which in turn leads to a lack of ownership by the workforce.

In this context it may not be irrelevant to consider modern-day Russia and Japan, the former decried for the quality of some of its products, the latter applauded. Yet no one could fault Russia for the theoretical standards it sets for its industries. And how many people realise how little emphasis is given by Japanese industry to external inspection? If quality is built into the production line, external inspection becomes almost superfluous.

This book will show the steps which need to be taken in order to 'build quality into the system'. Wherever possible, examples will be given, many based on the authors' experiences with Norfolk County Council

Norfolk began grappling with problems of quality in 1982, and in 1987 the Social Services Committee had the foresight to set up a Quality Control and Staff Development Section to be headed by an Assistant Director. This section incorporated the functions of training; inspection of all the Department's activities; advice on setting standards and interpreting legislation; homes registration and the inspection of statutory and independent homes to common criteria.

This section was to be fully integrated into the system of quality assurance. For example, Homes Registration Officers were involved in the drawing up of the *Revised Guide to Registration* and consulted homeowners about what should be included. They were to participate in training courses and seminars for the independent sector and, when required, would offer support and advice to isolated proprietors. In our view that was a far more effective way of raising levels of care than any threats to consider deregistration.

Norfolk evolved the vision of assuring the quality of all its services, not just of residential care. The tasks of the Unit inspecting residential homes are similar to those of staff who monitor home-care, occupational therapy and all aspects of fieldwork and day-care. Quality is an attitude of mind which should permeate throughout all the Department's activities, and it would be incongrous for residential care to have a different system from the rest of the Department.

We hope that this book will not be a disappointment to those who think that, by setting up an Inspection Unit, their quest for quality is complete. In our view, quality cannot be inspected into an organisation. Indeed, the present predilection for inspection could divert attention from the real issues surrounding quality unless they are put firmly into their proper contexts.

Much of what will be described could seem to some readers as nothing more than principles of sound management. So be it. Perhaps in essence that is what is lacking in many social care agencies. This book will attempt, however, to put these principles into a process which gives a high premium to consumer satisfaction, and ensures that staff are set objectives which are achievable.

Vested interests abound in the delivery of social care. In their time, professionals, managers, party political factions have held sway. More recently, it has been the day of the auditor and accountant. An emphasis on quality will at last put the consumer back in the picture. And, you never know, that might in the end prove agreeable to everyone.

Checklist of main points in Chapter One

1. Quality assurance is the responsibility of every person in an agency. This book sets out what *you* can do to achieve it.
2. Concentration on quality not only leads to satisfied users but it increases the job satisfaction of the workers and reduces costs to the employer.
3. To achieve quality, it is necessary to put it higher on the agenda than other cherished interests.
4. To do what the user wants, it may be necessary to lose some bureaucratic control.
5. There is no quick fix.
6. Setting standards and inspecting whether they are being achieved will not by themselves achieve quality.
7. Much of a quality assurance system can be described as good management.

2 From little acorns

The system of quality assurance which is to be described in this book began its life 9 years ago. To many, it was an unwanted baby, to be tolerated only because its parents were apparently respectable. During a disturbed and disturbing adolescence, not even its begetters were sure of what they had spawned, or whether their offspring would reach maturity.

This chapter logs the faultering steps which brought us to where we are today. Much of our thinking was empiric. Some was filched from elsewhere, including a clandestine visit to a 'bootiful' turkey-processing plant! Those readers who are confident that they have nothing to learn from the historical groping of others — or are just impatient — are welcome to pass on to Chapter 3!

In 1982, the management of Norfolk Social Services Department realised that it has a serious problem. It had no idea whether the services it was offering to the public were of a high enough quality. Management information consisted primarily of the volume, size and relative cost of various activities — but not whether they were effective or whether they were what the consumer wanted. True, the Department had detailed policies and procedures, which were constantly being revised by a team of social work consultants, but our performance review largely consisted on whether we received letters of complaint (and sometimes praise!) or what appeared in the local press, radio or television. When trying to evaluate if policies were being carried out, senior managers were almost totally reliant on the subjective views of middle managers and staff who were delivering the service. And the prime messages were: 'We need more staff' and 'We spend too much time on administration' and 'We are worse off than other parts of the organisation'. Do you recognise them?

The response was to appoint an inspector. Just one! He was to give independent assessments of performance both to senior managers and to the operators themselves.

Prior to the appointment, discussions had taken place with senior shop-stewards, and common ground was reached that the quality of social services activities should be beyond criticism in the interests of consumers and staff alike, and that too much emphasis in the past had been given to the costs of the service rather than its quality. The post was therefore advertised with full trade union backing.

Three difficulties immediately presented themselves:

- The task was too big for one person
- There were fears of the staff being inspected
- Against what standards was the inspector to measure performance?

It was decided that these difficulties could be overcome only by involving staff and trade unions in the whole exercise. A guarantee was given that information gathered as part of an inspection would not be used for disciplinary purposes — unless the member of staff subsequently refused to accept guidance or direction on how to improve. In each project undertaken, there would be an evaluation of the performance of managers as well as that of the operators. Each inspection would be carried out by a team comprising the inspector plus one or more operational staff, and it would be the first job of each team to draw up suggested standards which could be approved by management.

The involvement of operational staff in each inspection team was of particular importance. Not only did this ensure a bedrock of current reality to each inspection, but such peer group assessment — in the eyes of the 'inspected' — gave a credibility to the findings, which might well have been absent if all the inspectors had come from the ivory tower of County Hall. Staff were therefore seconded from their normal duties for up to 3 weeks. They were drawn from any level of responsibility and from fieldwork, residential, domiciliary or hospital sectors. The criteria used in their selection were that they were interested in the project, could be released from other duties for the duration of the inspection, and could bring realistic breadth of vision and understanding to the work. The staff themselves also invariably benefited, not only for the experience they gained but also from their feeling of being able to contribute something to the Department as a whole.

The simple formula used to prepare for the early inspections was to ask three basic questions. (But *please* remember that this was in the olden days of 10 years ago when quality assurance was still something to do with measuring engineering products! For a more sophisticated methodology, refer to Chapter 6 — Setting the standards.)

- What legislation gave mandatory or permissive powers for the activity to take place?
- What ministry circulars have been issued which affect the provision of service?
- What instructions had been given by managment regarding the quantity or quality of the service?

Following this, the team drew up a schedule of what it would be looking for during the inspection.

During the next 3 years, 22 inspections were carried out beginning with social enquiry reports, 'The role of team leaders', and 'What was going on in homes for elderly people' (during which inspectors lived in each of the 46 homes for 3 days in order to observe the regime). By 1985, it was possible to launch into an ambitious professional and administrative audit of all 12 teams of fieldworkers, a piece of work which earned the *Social Work Today* management award.

By then, it was time to take stock. We decided that the following lessons had been learned.

- Contrary to the fond belief of managment in the superiority of their procedures, staff did not really know what they were supposed to be doing. And, if it had not been made clear to staff what they were to do, it was difficult to criticise if they worked in a way of which the managers did not approve.
- When staff did know what they should be doing, they often had to choose to do something else because they had neither the time nor the tools to do a proper job. When the Department was under pressure, decisions on which work should have priority were often being taken by very junior staff.
- On the more positive side, the fact that inspections were now taking place was forcing managers into defining indicators and standards of quality.
- To announce what was going to be inspected immediately influenced priorities amongst the workers. No one wanted to be found lacking!
- Inspection, by itself, was not enough to promote quality. Being told that something was wrong did not, in itself, ensure that anyone would — or could — stop it from happening in future. Inspection needed to become part of the solution to the problems it identified, that is involved in defining achievable standards, training and developing the abilities of staff.
- Good-quality work could only come from workers who were properly motivated, directed and trained and who had time and confidence to do a proper job. Quality could not be inspected into the department. Control of quality must rest largely with the operators themselves and their immediate managers; spasmodic external inspections were too remote to have a lasting influence.
- Current views on what our 'clients' wanted were often patronising and sometimes wrong.

So, what was to be done? Like all good departments, when faced with a problem, *we re-organised!*

The new structure was based on four principles:

1. Decentralisation and the delegation to outposted units, not only responsibility for meeting client need but also control of resources to be able to do it. This means that each junior manager controlled the fieldwork, residential and domiciliary staff dealing with a particular client group in one locality.
2. Ensuring that no one was overwhelmed by having to tackle too wide a brief, a factor of particular importance in the light of the fundamental developments generated by *Care in the Community* and the *Children Act*. This was achieved by allocating both staff and management into one of three disciplines: families and children; elderly people; or disability.
3. Building quality into all aspects of our work, and creating a separate section to promote it (see Introduction).
4. Choosing boundaries which would enable the work of the Department to be delivered in concert with other agencies, both statutary and voluntary.

In view of what we will be saying later on in this book about the staff 'owning' what is happening in the agency, the way the restructuring was considered is of significance. The ideas and concepts underpinning it were discussed informally for well over 12 months in the usual meetings between senior and other members of staff. Indeed, such a length of time elapsed that a head of steam was generated amongst the workforce for 'something to happen'! That was the time to strike. But, even then, the preliminary report to the Social Services Committee was approved in principle only subject to consultation.

And the following consultations *did* make suggestions for change which was accepted by both management and committee. For example, the original proposal placed mental health in with services for families and children; staff, however, felt strongly that it would be better placed in the section helping people with physical or learning disabilities. Although the Director of Social Services thought that the staff were misguided, he agreed that the change should be made on the grounds that there was a better chance for a high-quality service if the staff were comfortable about the arrangements. Staff would feel that the service was more theirs.

But enough of restructuring. No doubt every department has a similar boring tale to tell!

Of more significance was the thinking which led to our present system of quality assurance, a system which, within reason, could be absorbed into any departmental structure. We consciously worked out, and studied, how the private manufacturing sector tried to achieve quality. Although accepting that the analogy was far from perfect, we were sure that there were lessons to be learned.

As an example, we took a car manufacturer. What steps would she/he have taken to produce a successful car? In simple terms, we lighted on the following stages:

1. They would have made absolutely sure what they were in the business of providing, and the principles on which it was going to be based. Were they to build a sports car or a runabout, a cheap economical vehicle, or a luxury one? For import or export? Environmentally friendly or performance dominated?

   In answering these questions, they would have researched the market into what gaps there were and what needs were perceived by the customer. They would also have borne in mind the restraints of current/future legislation and guidance, and the limits of their resources and resourcefulness.

   They would then turn this into an unambiguous statement of intent to guide themselves and their workers.
2. The car would be planned, and each stage of the manufacturing process would be clearly designed and fitted into the whole. Standards would be set for the quality of each part and the timescale in which it had to be produced. The standards would be based on what the customers would expect of the end product, e.g. plastic-covered seats might be acceptable in a runabout but not in a Rolls Royce.
3. It would then be necessary to set up an assembly line. Competent workers would be recruited and trained. The employers would ensure that the workforce knew what they had to do and that they were given the necessary tools. They would be given tasks which were achievable, and would be set standards by which they would know whether or not they were succeeding in their job. Above all, the workers would be motivated and given a pride in the worthiness of what they were doing.
4. When the prototype rolled off the assembly line, it would have a final inspection to see whether it met the standards for quality, cost and performance ordained in the original design. If it did not, changes would have to be made either in the design or in the way the assembly line was operating.
5. The car would then be marketed and an after-sales service provided. In other words, the manufacturer would tell people about the new car, and deal with any justified complaints or defects.
6. The main test of success would be whether customers wanted to buy the car. There is no point in designing and producing something even to the highest quality when no one wants it. If there is consumer dissatisfaction or apathy, the manufacturer would try to find out the reason, learn by the mistake and go back to the drawing-board.
7. The whole manufacturing process would be reviewed regularly in order to comply with customer wishes and changes in legal

requirements. There would be a constant search for improvement.

Using this basic model, flawed as it no doubt is, we designed the process of quality assurance which is described in subsequent chapters of this book. Not being too arrogant to learn further from others, however, the Assistant Director in charge of the Department's Quality Section made a number of visits to successful firms to discover what they thought to be important.

Marks and Spencer provided us with a key focus, i.e. the customer. All services were geared as a priority to ensuring that she/he would be satisfied. In so doing, it became apparent that other interested groups (e.g. staff, suppliers and investors) became satisfied as well.

The second important lesson came from a visit to a Bernard Matthews' turkey factory. Visting incognito, the new Assistant Director described his experience in an issue of the magazine *Insight* of 1.8.90.

> 'My visit was a marvellously revealing experience. The factory had all the usual quality checks and procedures, but there was something more. It may not have been much consolation to the turkey, but each one was prepared with care and even pride. Every member of staff was responsible and accountable for the quality of the task he or she was assigned to do.
>
> 'Their tasks were not checked; they were responsible themselves for the quality of the product. The managers had a reminder system in operation whereby they reminded each operator to monitor their own work. Each individual worker was not only responsible for their work, but they were also fully accountable for the quality of the tasks they were performing.
>
> 'By adding an accountability factor to their trading skill, workers committed themselves more and more, and they intuitively established their ownership of their assigned tasks. The workforce was relaxed and responsible: there was positive group pressure on workers. "Any worker who was performing badly would not survive in an environment where everyone was striving for good quality," said one team leader in the factory.
>
> 'One of the key objectives of community care in the next decade and beyond is to clarify the responsibilities of agencies and their workers to make it easier to hold them to account for their performance. The factory appeared to have achieved this important objective.'

So, added to the framework of what we thought a car manufacturer might do to achieve quality were the principles of Marks and Spencer and Bernard Matthews: the service needed to be consumer-oriented and staff needed to 'own' the quality of what they were doing. How was it to be done? Read on!

Checklist of main points in Chapter Two

1. To set up a successful quality assurance system, it is necessary to involve staff and trade unions at the beginning of the exercise.
2. Information gathered as part of the process should be used to seek improvements to the service, and not be used for disciplinary purposes.
3. Inspections should evaluate the performance of managers and policy makers as well as the operators.
4. It is beneficial to co-opt front-line workers on to inspection teams.
5. Good-quality work can only come from workers who are properly motivated and trained, and who have time and confidence to do a proper job.
6. The basic system of quality assurance used in Norfolk is based on how a good car would be produced.

- Vision and Mission Statement
- Design of vehicle and service
- Setting of standards
- Creation of the assembly line
- Inspection of the end product
- After-sales service and dealing with complaints
- Ascertainment of the wishes of consumers at all stages
- Regular review and refinements.

3 What is this thing, quality assurance?

Those of you who have kept with us for the first two chapters will already have a fair idea of the answer. But two simple snappy definitions of the aims of a quality assurance system are given below.

> *'Quality Assurance is making sure that the users of a service always get what they have been promised.'*

> *'To get things right first time and every-time without picking up expensive or embarrassing mistakes at the end of the day.'*

This obviously begs the question: 'getting it right for whom?' Is it the people who set out to provide the service in the first place, or the workforce, or the consumer? Who is it that has to be satisfied about the quality of service? It will come as no surprise, when we say that, in theory, all have to be satisfied. In practice, this is hard to achieve. But, if one or more parties to this contract are confused and discontented, a quality service will not be delivered, and the ensuing conflict invariably ensures that the others become dissatisfied as well.

Somehow, the inspirations of designer, operator and consumer have to become congruent before a product can be delivered which is accepted by all involved as being of the required quality. It is futile for a producer to deliver a service which the consumer does not want, or at a level which the consumer finds unacceptable. Likewise, there is no point in the consumer complaining that he is not receiving something which the producer has not set out to deliver. And, even if producer and consumer do agree on the level of service to be provided, a satisfactory quality will not be achieved unless the workforce wants to deliver it and is enabled so to do.

The business of quality assurance is to ensure that the service which is offered at the point of delivery to a consumer meets the standards which have been set by the designer and which are seen as acceptable by the consumer.

A more formal definition is to be found in Chapter 5 of 'Purchase of service', the practice guidance issued by the Social Services inspectorate:

> 'Quality assurance is used to refer to those processes which aim to ensure that concern for quality is designed and built in to services. It implies commitment on the part of local social service committee members and senior managers to a systematic approach to the pursuit of quality and will be demonstrated by an explicit statement of policy, setting out agency expectations and standards. Systematic and comprehensive arrangements to ensure that the required standards are achieved will be evident throughout organisational procedures and will include processes for verification and feedback.
>
> 'Quality control refers to those processes of verification and will include systematic monitoring, including statistical and other management information, recurring and one-off audits and inspection activity designed to establish whether standards are being achieved. Quality control is one aspect of quality assurance. It should provide objective feedback to line managers, who have continuing responsibility for quality, about what is actually being achieved.
>
> 'Total quality management (TQM) describes an approach to quality assurance which stresses the importance of creating a culture in which concern for quality is an integral part of service delivery. This means there is ownership of responsibility for the quality of services at all levels of the organisation and involvement of staff in the pursuit of clear and explicit quality objectives.'

Anne Parker, C.B.E., the Director of Social Services for the Royal County of Berkshire, gave the following definition of quality assurance to a Department of Health sponsored conference:

> 'Quality assurance is an umbrella term for a continuous process of organisational development and improvement, building on current strengths and good practices, and using new tools and techniques to develop more systematic and disciplined methods of work.
>
> 'Our aim in Berkshire is to create a climate of innovation and development, where staff feel motivated to assess the quality of their service and improve it — which involves everyone.'

This is a definition which the authors endorse wholeheartedly. In fact, the bulk of this book will be debating and refining the concepts contained in it.

'Quality' may mean different things to different people. To the councillor or owner, a main requirement may be value for money. The manager, on the other hand, may have as a priority that his/her policy objectives are achieved, or legal requirements met. The consumer wants his problem solved to his satisfaction, whether or not the method meets the aspirations of managers or is cost effective.

We are again indebted to Anne Parker and Hugh Dunnachie of Berkshire County Council for the following examples of how quality is seen.

- Research by a major bank into what its customers saw as constituting 'quality' revealed that they wanted a service which was: reliable, consistent, responsive, accurate, competent, accessible, courteous, willing and able to communicate in an understandable way, trustworthy, secure, confidential, understanding and delivered in surroundings which made them feel comfortable.

- Questioning councillors about what they were interested in showed that their attention was excited by: where things have gone wrong, value for money, local issues, competitive tendering, local political considerations. Management showed a greater interest in: difficulties in delivering services, time constraints, the national political situation, budget constraints, and gaining political consensus.

The purpose of a quality assurance system is to ensure that the differing interests and aspirations of provider and user are met.

For this to be achieved, such a culture must be absorbed throughout all of an organisation, and the actions to maintain it must become an integral part of the staff's day-to-day operation. And by 'staff' we mean absolutely everyone who contributes in any way to a particular process. It is easy to accept that those in face-to-face contact with the consumer deal with them courteously and efficiently, but for an organisation to be truly quality minded, the same principal applies to those who may never see a member of the public.

It would be a mistake to put the total thrust of your quality assurance activity into those people who actually meet the users of the service. Important though that is, those face-to-face workers are dependent themselves on receiving a quality service from their own 'background' people.

There is a lovely story — perhaps apochryphal — about an airline which was transporting a group of holiday-makers from the United States to London. Unfortunately the luggage of half the passengers was sent by mistake to Tokyo. The airline showed appropriate concern. Hostesses grovelled, free drinks were dispensed, and the passengers were provided with toilet requisites and underwear to last until the baggage was recovered — some 4 days later. Towards the end of the holiday, each passenger was asked to fill in a questionnaire about their level of satisfaction with the service. Believe it or believe it not, the passengers who had received the concerned attention of the hostesses because their luggage had gone astray, showed more satisfaction that those who had their baggage all the time but who had felt out of things. The airline was delighted with the success of its 'consumer care' policy. But the saga did not finish there. When the holiday-makers arrived back in New York, those who had originally lost their baggage found that it had been again sent to Tokyo. No amount of 'consumer care' could mollify those passengers. And a second questionnaire seeking the views of all the passengers on the satisfaction they felt, led to quite different conclusions!

This little story gives us three important messages:

1. Quality assurance is much more than being nice to people and hoping that they have a good day!
2. A quality assurance system must involve all people in an organisation — the baggage handlers are just as important in delivering quality as the airline manager and the flight crew.
3. If a mistake occurs — and it will from time to time, no matter how good your preparation — the quality assurance system must be able to identify the cause and make speedy corrections to ensure that it is not repeated.

May we refer you to one of the two snappy definitions set out at the beginning of this chapter: 'to get things right first time and every-time without picking up expensive or embarrassing mistakes'. Perhaps we do not really have to spell out the cost to an organisation of having to keep correcting faults, (although we do admit that such a scenario is better than the organisation that makes mistakes and does *not* correct them!) We will, however, list a few of the costs:

- duplication of effort, i.e. the work is done twice over;
- having to waste time dealing with the complaint;
- perhaps having to pay compensation;
- a lowering of staff morale and motivation;
- developing a bad reputation.

Let us take another example a little nearer home and consider who is involved in providing a quality service for someone living in a residential home for elderly people. Obviously, the care staff must be sensitive at all times to the wishes and preferences of the resident; and it is not too hard for that also to be seen as necessary by domestic and kitchen staff. But how the resident views the standard of care offered might also depend on the person who is dealing with how much she/he is being assessed to pay, a person in a large organisation who may never see a resident. To receive an incomprehensible letter in response to a query — or even worse, no letter at all — is hardly likely to enhance the consumer's satisfaction. And what of the other 'officials' who routinely visit the home — the architect, the workman, the decorator — do they treat the resident with dignity and do they respect the privacy and timescales of an elderly person?

Poor service can be given by a range of different service givers, and the 'cost' of that poor service damages the organisation trying to deliver care. Quality has to be 'absorbed' not only by all the staff of a department or agency, but also by those on whom those staff have to rely in order to deliver a comprehensive service. Now, that would be a good topic to put on the agenda of the Chief Officers' Group!

Norfolk defined its quality objectives in the following way, and will insist on their being met by outside contractors as well as by directly employed staff:

- a client-focused service;
- a service which satisfies the needs of consumers most appropriately by involving them in the decision-making process;
- a prompt and appropriate response to consumer requests throughout the county;
- the most effective and imaginative use of available resources for the benefit of consumers.

Those objectives cannot be delivered however without enlisting the ownership of quality by the workforce, an ownership which can only be guaranteed if individual workers throughout the organisation are given the responsibility and accountability for the tasks they perform. A prime task of a quality assurance system is to ensure that staff embrace that those objectives wholeheartedly and have the competence to deliver them.

And that means *all* staff. If we may quote the deputy general secretary of the Social Care Association, Des Kelly, in an interview with *Care Weekly:* 'I think it is a real travesty that the people expected to provide care for the most needy members of society are those most poorly paid and with the least opportunities for training. It is important for people who are care assistants to realise how much impact they have and how important they are. They can make the difference in the current rhetoric about quality. They can make the resident happy from day to day.'

A quality service will not be offered by someone who does not appreciate fully the worth or value of the job they are doing, and know how it affects what the whole organisation is trying to do. That includes support staff just as much as the more publicised front-line troups. A clerk supporting the homecare service is just as important as the homecare assistant herself, for, if messages are not recorded efficiently or time sheets are delayed, at the end of the day the service to the consumer will be adversely affected. One of the challenges of management is to ensure that this attitude percolates the dim recesses of other departments and agencies, especially Treasury, Personnel and Supplies, who may not realise how their inflexibility or tardiness reflects on how the consumer views the home-help or social worker.

Ownership by staff requires them to have enough responsibility and pride in their job to check the quality of what they themselves are doing rather than leaving the faults to be found out by someone else. A quality assurance system ensures that, not only are staff capable of accepting that responsibility (as they were in the turkey factory described in Chapter 2), but it controls the standards actually being achieved through continuous monitoring and inspection. A word of warning, however:

inspection is but one part of the quality assurance process. By itself, it can only make an appraisal of the standard of care being offered. For any deficiencies in that standard of care to be rectified, there needs to be present the complementary assistance of training, problem-solving, policy formulation and a personnel strategy which will deliver a sufficient workforce. In particular, the training and development of *all* staff will give the organisation a vitality and competence without which quality will be difficult to achieve.

In labour-intensive organisations like social care agencies, human resources are amongst the most important assets. The competence and motivation of the workforce are crucial for success. Unless the skills, imagination and commitment of the staff are unlocked and cherished, we can say farewell to our vision of quality. The development of task-centred and competency-based training must be the corner-stone of the push to improve quality during the nineties. This requires not only a general commitment by management, but a personal involvement and constant interest which can be seen by staff as a measure of the importance of the issue. The encouragement for staff to take time from their jobs to undertake training is too fundamental to leave to hard-pressed junior managers. The commitment of senior managers is much more than trying to obtain adequate funding.

Staff knowing what they are supposed to be doing is patently a pre-requisite for the successful carrying out of the agency's aspirations. Understandable and achievable policies and procedures therefore play a vital role in the quality assurance process. Are you satisfied that your procedures are user friendly? Or have they been written with a view of covering the backsides of management when things go wrong? A lesson learned in Norfolk some 10 years ago was that, if staff do not find their instructions easy to understand, they tend to adapt them and make up their own, which may or may not comply with the Mission Statement of their agency and which may lack a consistent professional approach.

Before we leave our description of what we believe are the main ingredients of quality assurance, perhaps we should also deal with one common fallacy. Because the word 'quality' has been purloined by manufacturers of expensive goods, there is a danger of assuming that quality is synonymous with being expensive. This is not so.

Expense only comes into the equation if the standards which have been promised to the user are costly to achieve. And, just because a great deal of money is spent on trying to reach those standards, it does not mean that quality is assured. No doubt we all know of instances where expensive equipment or services have failed to deliver — computer systems are a prime example.

In terms of quality assurance, quality is achieved if the standards agreed between provider and user are actually met. Those standards may be either costly or inexpensive. That is immaterial. What is at issue is what the users have been promised and what they are expecting. For example, the purchaser of a Reliant Robin can be just as satisfied with the quality of the product as someone who buys a Rolls Royce. He does not expect electric windows, leather upholstery and a top speed of 150 miles per hour. And when he does not get them, he is therefore not unhappy. He would only complain about the quality if, for example, it was scratched on delivery or it broke down — just as indeed would be the owner of a new Rolls.

So, that is quality assurance. Why do we bother?

The simple answer is that if such a system is put into operation, everyone has the potential to benefit:

- The councillor will be in control of policy and will be reassured that the resources allocated to the service will be used in the most cost-effective way.
- Managers will control the standards that are to be set and will know the outcomes of everybody's efforts.
- Staff will have the time, space and equipment to do a proper job, and will be consulted about how the service can be improved.
- Users will receive the service which has been agreed with them and in a way which satisfies them.

Checklist of main points in Chapter Three

1. Two definitions of quality assurance:

   - Quality assurance is making sure that the users of a service always get what they have been promised.
   - To get things right first time and every time without picking up expensive or embarrassing mistakes at the end of the day.

2. Somehow, the aspirations of designer, operator and consumer have to become congruent before a product or service can be delivered which is accepted by all involved as being of the required quality.
3. The business of quality assurance is to ensure that the service which is offered at the point of delivery to a consumer meets the standards which have been set by the designer and which are seen as acceptable by the consumer.
4. The ultimate duty of promoting the milieu in which quality can flourish must rest with the producer, the home owner, the Council — whoever has responsibility for delivering the product or service.
5. The responsive — and successful — producer will listen to the workforce and the consumers before deciding on a level of service.
6. The objectives of an agency cannot be delivered without enlisting the ownership of quality by *all* the workforce, an ownership which can only be guaranteed if individual workers throughout the organisation are given responsibility and accountability for the tasks they perform.
7. Unless the skills, imagination and commitment of staff are unlocked and cherished, we can say farewell to our vision of quality.
8. 'Quality' is not synonymous with high cost, and should not be confused with only being nice to consumers.
9. Quality assurance benefits councillor/owner, manager, staff and user.
10. Any failures or deficiencies in service should be rectified to prevent them being repeated.

4 Creating the right climate

To a large extent, the task of management to work out a quality assurance system is not a particularly difficult one. The biggest challenge is to create the right climate amongst the whole workforce to ensure that what has been planned is actually put into practice. For, despite the best endeavours of senior staff, the success or failure of a quality system depends on the actions of all staff in the agency, not just those who have the responsibility for devising new patterns of working. Put bluntly, you will never deliver a quality service if your workforce is suspicious, demoralised, and sees its management as a hindrance rather than a help.

And the responsibility for establishing this climate rests squarely on the shoulders of management. Yes, you may believe that you have an awkward workforce or that the trade unions are difficult and obstructive, but, in general, management gets the industrial relations it deserves. It is a truism that the responsibility for managing lies with management.

Senior management (and councillors) have to make a planned and continuing contribution to sustaining the morale of their staff. High morale just doesn't appear or disappear. It has to be worked for. Time has to be spent on it. The subject should be high on the agenda at all times, and not just addressed when a problem is perceived. In particular, 'macho' management and councillors should be wary lest the smack of strong management destroys rather than supports the mutual trust and confidence which is necessary if the service user is to receive the best service available. The same can be said of trade unions.

From the Norfolk experience, we found that the following five aspects need to be addressed in order to establish a positive climate and style:

- Enthusiasm
- Imagination
- Maximisation
- Consultation
- Pride

Let us spend a few minutes examining each of them.

Enthusiasm

In the commercial world there is a saying, 'An unenthusiastic person should not open a shop'. Enthusiasm is infectious. It attracts confidence. Service users will interact more easily with a worker who is enthusiastic. Such a worker presents a good image of the agency. If your service is to be 'user centred', a primary objective should be to kindle and sustain enthusiasm amongst the staff.

The converse is revealed by a complaint received by one of the authors from an elderly person who was unable to cope at home even with the maximum of domiciliary support. When she asked that she be considered for residential care, the response she received from her social worker led her to ring up the local manager to ask: 'Do they not include enthusiasm and courtesy in the syllabus of professional training for social workers?'

Luckily, most people beginning a career in one of the social care agencies (like shopkeepers!) are enthusiastic, and are motivated by their desire to help people overcome whatever is hindering them to lead as full a life as possible. But, just as many small shopkeepers are dispirited because of high business rates and other financial disincentives, so staff in social care agencies can lose their drive and enthusiasm unless they think they are valued and respected by the agency.

Without wishing to appear too negative to the reader, we do think it necessary to consider briefly five influences which management will have to consider sensitively if they are not to lead to a demoralised workforce.

The pace of change

Agencies are having to cope with the *Children Act*, The *NHS and Community Care Act*, restrictions on expenditure, care management, the purchaser/provider split, possible contracting out of services, changes in the health services, education reforms. Senior management and councillors are heavily involved in redesigning service delivery. How is this being seen by the rest of the staff in the agency?

Henry Ford came up with a wise saying: 'If it ain't bust, then don't fix it'.

Committees and senior managers would do well to heed that advice. Despite the theoretical basis for many of the proposed changes and restructurings, too much upheaval is counter-productive, not only in the short term but in the long term as well. Unless the workforce is fully engaged in the positive reasons for doing things differently, change will be seen negatively as criticism of their present performance. Restructurings will be regarded as 'theirs' and not 'ours'.

There is no simple remedy. Remember, any changes dreamed up by management have to be absorbed by the rest of the staff *in addition* to what they are already doing. The slow process of consultation prior to Norfolk's restructuirng (see Chapter 2) could be taken as a model.

Our advice, therefore, is threefold.

- Do not make changes unless you have to, especially if there is no evidence of poor performance. There are already enough legal imperatives to cope with.
- Unless you have a legal deadline to meet, don't make changes until all staff have had the opportunity to absorb the reasons and to work out the consequences.
- Do not expect the same people to be involved in too many changes at once. Many departments have already moved into specialist social workers. We suggest that you consider creating specialist managers as well.

Staff shortages

We are not so naive as to believe that it is possible for senior managers to guarantee full staff establishments. But it has to be accepted that shortages of staff can lead to the strongest beliefs amongst the workforce that 'those up there don't care about us'. But there are three dispiriting factors that can be overcome.

First, the length of time it takes in some agencies to advertise and appoint new staff. In one authority no less than 29 processes had to be undertaken before a care assistant or home-help could be replaced — and this when the person resigning only had to give 1 weeks' notice! In actual fact, the shortest possible time for all the procedures to be carried out was 4 months. And what was supposed to be happening in the meantime? We strongly urge you to look at your own procedures to ensure that replacements can be processed without bureaucratic delay. In addition, have you clear speedy directions about what can be done to replace people on sick leave?

Secondly, the expectation by some senior managers that the same level of service will be delivered even though the full complement of staff is not present. Indeed, we have heard one Director of Social Services say — when his area team of social workers was 30 per cent down in numbers — that he left, to local discretion, the work which needn't be carried out. In our view there is a clear difference between delegation and abrogation of responsibility. It was interesting to listen to the views of his staff, who were worried sick about what would happen to them if something went wrong with a case and they had cut corners in the procedures which had been laid down. We believe that it is the task of senior managers and councillors at times of staff shortages to 'come up front' and spell out to staff and general public alike what services are having to be curtailed. At least their staff may be able to do a proper job with what remains. Nothing diminishes enthusiasm more than believing you have an impossible job and that you will get it in the neck when things go wrong.

Thirdly, when there is little likelihood of attracting sufficient, qualified staff within a reasonable time, has management reassessed what work presently being carried out by trained workers could be transferred to people without formal qualifications — at least for a temporary period? Several years ago, an evaluation of the work in Norfolk of social workers approved under the Mental Health Act showed that much of their time was spent on problems concerned with welfare benefits, accommodation and employment, some of which could have been done just as effectively by unqualified staff. We suspect that some of the tasks undertaken in the childcare field could also be transferred to a welfare assistant working in close conjunction with the social worker. Rather than having vacancies and work left undone, look at how much could be done by people without formal qualifications. The remaining staff may well feel more enthusiastic about their job if they can spend more time on the tasks for which they have been trained.

Inadequate training

It is a truism to state that the greatest resources in any labour-intensive organisation are the people employed in it. And it follows that, if the agency is to maximise that resource, it has to ensure that all staff work to their full potential. Few people would quarrel with the concept that each member of staff should have a personal framework of training appropriate for their development. Indeed, a comprehensive staff development programme is a great motivating factor for staff — and a good recruitment tool as well. Enthusiasm is lost, however, if the agency is not prepared to fund the necessary training programme or cannot release a member of staff because of vacant posts. It is easy for senior staff to say 'no' for short-term reasons. But, will the user in the longer term get a quality service from dispirited, frustrated — and possibly underskilled — staff?

Control

We acknowledge that management must be allowed to state clearly what it expects the workforce to achieve, and that staff are only employed to deliver services in line with those directions. But, within that rubric, management attitudes can determine whether staff learn to do what is expected through a process of enabling, support and encouragement, or whether they are prevented from doing wrong things by a system relying on policing, checks, referral upwards of minor decisions. The latter will inevitably lead to 'defensive' work based on a fear of making a mistake. The former can bring out initiative and enthusiasm. Which attitude does your agency promote? And by 'agency' we include the strictures which may be put on staff by those in control of finance and personnel issues. But more of this later.

In this context, we would reiterate our warning about excessive reliance on inspection as a prime method of control. Quite simply, inspection by itself does little to improve the quality of service delivery. Higher performance will only come from a workforce which owns and controls its own quality.

Accommodation and facilities

Poor accommodation and conditions of service will lead staff to believe that management does not value them. Not only will morale fall, but these deficiencies will probably lead to difficulties in recruitment and retention. National conditions of service do limit the scope of manoeuvring open to management on pay, but there is plenty of latitude in respect of office accommodation and facilities. (But more of this in Chapter 7.)

So much for factors which could lead to staff becoming dispirited and demotivated. What positive steps can management take to promote enthusiasm? The next four headings in this chapter will cover areas which will help, but in addition there are two other qualities that management could show which could encourage their workforce into fighting with them rather than against them.

The first quality — somewhat tritely — is leadership. It is unlikely that staff will show enthusiasm for their jobs if they are led by people they do not know, do not trust, do not understand, and perhaps even fear.

The examples shown by national politicians towards various parts of their domain is enlightening. Look back to the Gulf War. The Secretary of State for Defence seemed to be constantly in the Middle East, meeting the troops and telling them: 'You are doing a fine job. We are all behind you. Whatever you need to succeed, it will be provided. We are proud of you.' The Prime Minister made a similar visit and expressed similar views.

Contrast that with the way in which recent Secretaries of State for Health of all parties have 'encouraged' their own front-line troops. (Yes, we know that the Government does not actually employ directly the people it expects to implement its social care legislation, but in the 'war' against abuse, deprivation and neglect, the only foot soldiers they have are us!) When did you last hear the staff in social care agencies being praised and stimulated by their national political leaders? Rather, they are ignored and rounded upon when, on occasion, things go wrong. One gets the impression that Social Services are seen as somewhat distasteful — like drains: 'I suppose we have to have them, but there is no need to like them — or even talk about them'.

Style of leadership will set the culture of an organisation. A decision on the culture required should be taken *before* the leadership style is put into place. Do you want a 'tight ship' where the staff will be conditioned to do as they are told, where keeping the budget under strict control has the utmost priority, where deviations from the set pattern are dealt with via the disciplinary procedures? It *can* be done with a combination of authority, command and fear of reprisal. Others may prefer a style which encourages initiative, believing that the benefits of harnessing all the talents of the workforce will outweigh the potential problems posed by delegation of authority and control.

Once the style has been put in place, senior managers have to work hard at sustaining it — and this is where many managements fail their staff. The responsibilities of senior Social Services staff are threefold: to advise their Council on all matters relating to social services, to contribute to the corporate running of the authority, and to manage the Department in a way which will best deliver the policies of the Council. At times of great change, there is a pull on senior staff to concentrate on the first two functions and to neglect their responsibilities to their own workforce. And that neglect may change the culture of the Department.

In order to have confidence in the abilities of their managers and to be able to trust them with their problems and difficulties, staff need to know them. The very minimum is that they can put faces to names! Personal contact is important. It is difficult for staff to give their loyalty to an anonymous leadership. An even greater problem which a 'remote' management will face is that staff will look elsewhere than their managers for resolution of their problems — to other colleagues, trade unions, opposition councillors, the media and *in extremis* to organisations representing users. Such anarchy will destroy whatever culture management is hoping to engender.

So, the first positive action that can be taken to sustain enthusiasm amongst staff is to offer a style of leadership consistent with the culture you wish to promote, and to work hard at maintaining it. You, senior managers and councillors, show your faces to your staff. Debate with them. Show interest in what your staff are doing. Praise. In large geographical areas, cultivate the media; as a second best, it does the Department's image no harm to be seen as people of interest. Above all, become *people* rather than just names at the bottom of memoranda. Staff can give loyalty to managers whom they think they know and can trust. Absentee managers breed cynicism.

The second quality to show is to ensure that all staff are treated and valued in the same way as you would wish yourself to be. Consider what makes you feel good about your job and what dispirits you, and make sure that the organisation promotes whatever is helpful and eliminates factors which hinder. Even better than doing this from personal experience would be to ask the staff themselves — but before you do that you must be prepared to act positively about their complaints, or at least explain thoroughly why things cannot change. Few things can alienate staff more than management failing to respond speedily and incisively to the ideas or complaints. A positive, responsive and enthusiastic management is far more likely to have an enthusiastic workforce than one which is constantly wrapped up in problems which seem pretty peripheral to the difficulties that staff face in trying to deliver a quality service.

Imagination

The second feature of the style which we decided to try to promote in Norfolk is imagination — or perhaps flair and initiative are better descriptions.

As every problem presented by the Department's users is unique, workers have to be imaginative to provide responsive client-centred solutions. Although the basic knowledge may have to be common, every problem has to be addressed differently.

It is not easy, however, for people to be imaginative as a matter of course. And imagination can so easily be stifled by restrictive managers. A few years ago *Readers Digest* described a small piece of research, where a teacher went to a group of adults at a further education class, and, putting a black dot on the board, asked them to identify it. It was not a catch question, and everyone said it was a black dot. The teacher then repeated the experiment with a group of youngsters between the ages of six and ten at a primary school. When he asked them to identify the black dot, there was at first a silence. Then an arm was raised and a confident voice declared that it was a Mexican hat. An immediate protest was launched by another child, who insisted that it looked more like burnt hamburgers. A third youngster believed that it represented a squashed fly.

Children are imaginative. Adults tend to lose that faculty. As was stated in the paper produced in 1977 by the National Children's Bureau, where children in care gave their views: 'Unfortunately some adults listen "with one ear blocked", for they have lost the sensitivity of childhood.'

Of course, we are not recommending that staff can put into effect any wild idea that may come into their minds. Imagination and flair must be firmly based in knowledge — sound professional training and clear directives about the standards and values which the agency finds acceptable. But within those limits, innovation is to be encouraged.

To promote this, in 1988 Norfolk created a structure which combined delegation with flexibiity. To take services for elderly people as an example, one team manager would manage all the Department's resources for elderly people in a locality. She/he had at her disposal one or two residential homes, daycare facilities, Homecare Organiser and

Home-Carers, social workers and assistants and a budget for promoting voluntary activity. The manager's task was to use any of these resources to assess social needs in the locality, and to use them flexibly in any way she wanted in order to satisfy those needs.

The idea behind this model was to free up the thinking of all staff and to encourage them to identify with both the problems and the solutions to them. We had learned our lessons from the splitting of fieldwork, residential care and day-care in the early 1970s, which led to so much conflict and passing the buck from one section to another.

The manager still had to remain within the overall cash limit allocated to her, but we were striving — with some success — to enable her to spend that money imaginatively for the benefit of the service users. In our view this is just as effective a way of controlling the budget as checking that every item of expenditure is within limits for which prior approval has been sought and given. And, when user demand is outstripping resources, we believe that this approach will give the best value for money and offer the best quality service. To cap it all, staff using their imagination and initiative are enthusiastic and committed.

Maximisation

The most effective use of resources is fundamental to the concept of quality assurance. It is certainly a powerful selling point with politicians! And yet few local authorities have a structure which allows this to happen. Social care agencies tend to compartmentalise. Budget estimates are fixed in stone. To switch money or staff from one activity to another is a job worthy of Sysiphus. You cannot do something unless the money has been assigned to it — perhaps 18 months beforehand. Initiatives are stifled. We are often on a train which cannot change its destination even when we would choose to go somewhere else. At a time of severe financial restraint, it may seem incongrous to suggest a blurring of the boundaries between areas of agreed expenditure, but, unless treasurers can be persuaded that there is more to delivering social care than keeping to the agreed minutiae of the budget book, many of the resources available will be too inflexible to meet the needs of users.

Just as important as money is time. We have already given examples above of how qualified staff were being used inappropriately. How many other tasks in the agency are being carried out by over-qualified staff? How much of the work, for example, of occupational therapists and social workers can be done by assistants and helpers? And how much staff time is spent in meetings? Even though we accept the necessity of properly structured team meetings, do you ever work out the salary costs of some of the meetings that are held, and ask whether the time and money could be better spent? We know of some area teams (outside Norfolk we are pleased to say!) which still cling to the cosiness of weekly allocation meetings.

Irrespective of the time they divert from face-to-face contact with users, we challenge those who still hold these meetings to ask the users if they think their best interests are being served by waiting a few days until the whole team discusses who should deal with them.

On the other hand, staff need the protection of having a workload which is manageable. Overload leads to inefficiency and mistakes. Mistakes are expensive. If one of the aims of quality assurance is to get things done right first time, and every time, in order to forstall expensive mistakes, then overloaded staff will fail. Staff can only work at their optimum if their tasks and goals are achievable. A workload management system protects both the worker and the agency.

But perhaps the most effective way of making the best of the resources available is to think afresh with your staff about the way that things are being done and who is doing them. Wherever possible, involve the private and voluntary sectors as well.

The three examples which we are about to give are neither unique nor all-embracing. They are merely ways in which one local authority used a little lateral and flexible thinking in order to overcome the straight-jacket of restricted resources. They are given mainly to show an attitude of mind, which it was hoped would run through the whole Department. For we must expect managers — as well as other staff members — to maximise resources!

First, the expansion of daycare services without building new centres. This was for two reasons — because the Government would not allow the County Council to borrow the money for a new building, but also because it seemed odd to us that, although we had a policy of integrating people into the local community, one of the first things we did if they required care or stimulation was to segregate them!

So, training centres were used as a base from which attenders were placed with private employers, adult education classes, voluntary agencies such as play-groups, clubs for elderly people — even the local football club. Over 200 placements were created and sustained by seven extra staff, a solution which was better for users, cheaper for the County Council, and which used to the full not only the Department's facilities but also those available in the community.

For elderly people — especially in the more rural areas — day-care was expanded by placements with families, on the same principle as child-minding. If it is good enough for children, why is it not good enough for older people? Other placements were found in residential homes run by the independent sector. Why bus an old person many miles to a County Council daycare centre, when there is a residential home in the same village? And, if someone requires a meal at lunch-time, what is wrong with the local pub?

For those with mental health problems and those who may require counselling or daytime activity, staff were appointed to work peripatetically. Users were not stigmatised by being brought into a new centre. The staff used the same facilities as the rest of the community, and if they required a meeting place for activities such as group-work, they agreed with the users the most appropriate facility and then hired it. Again, no costly building to finance and maintain.

The second example works on similar lines to the first. Why do we need to provide new residential hostels? Care can be given by staff without herding them into an expensive building. By using flats and bedsits offered by local councils, housing associations and the private sector, residents were supported by the same numbers of staff as would have been needed to look after residents in a residential home. Cover could be provided on a shift system, as in a residential home, and someone could be on call after 10 o'clock at night. This system is used primarily for youngsters about to leave care, for people with mental health problems, and for young offenders on bail who don't then have to be remanded in expensive custody.

The third example utilises the skill of residential workers to the best advantage. Instead of having an artificial split between residential care and fieldwork, residential workers were used as key workers to support in the community those children and adults who once lived with them. They also gave practical advice to foster parents, for who in the Department would know better than residential wokers how to handle the problems posed by difficult children? They have knowledge and experience beyond that of many fieldworkers. Why not use it?

Maximise the effect of any facility you have at your disposal, and don't get too hung up on who does what.

Consultation

A proper and honest consultation process is an asset not only in good customer care but also in good-quality management. So the fourth aspect we considered necessary when trying to creåte a climate in which quality could thrive was to encourage staff at all levels to listen and to respond.

And just as social care workers should consult with service users before deciding on the best way of helping them with their problems, so management of an agency needs to listen to its staff before deciding on the most appropriate methods of delivering services. There is no real alternative if the staff are to 'own' their work practices.

Of course, what we have just said is old hat. No one would really disagree. The problem is putting it into practice.

Let us give you a couple of examples. For many years Norfolk has had a policy that children of appropriate age and their parents should be involved in the statutory 6-month review meetings, which review a child's progress and plan for the future. A survey, however, of reviews showed that in practice less than 15 per cent of parents and children were involved. Social workers had not really absorbed the thinking behind the policy, and were making little effort to put it into practice. What is more, they could come up with a plethora of reasons why the policy was inappropriate in that particular case! In fact, the policy was being seen as another hurdle to overcome rather than an integral part of good social work practice. There had been a failure of management to consult, discuss and persuade before sending out the instruction. Let us hasten to add that this happened many years ago, before the *Children Act* was even thought of!

A second example involves a chair-bound old lady attending a day-centre for the first time. When one of the authors asked if she was happy coming to the centre, she lowered her voice and said that it was not what she really wanted, but she did not wish to upset her social worker, who was 'a very nice lady and had been very helpful to her'. With a bit of encouragement, the elderly lady explained. Before she had become completely housebound about 6 months ago, she used to meet her friends twice a week in the city for a cup of tea and a chat. That was her main social outing, and she used to look forward to it with a great deal of pleasure. When she became unable to get out of the house, she became depressed and the doctor suggested a social work visit. The social worker visited her promptly, and speedily arranged for the lady to attend the day centre five times per week without really ascertaining what she really wanted. The lady felt overwhelmed and grateful, but was too shy to express her wishes. Indeed, she was not given an opportunity so to do. And yet, with flexible thinking and budgets, it would not have been difficult to provide the lady with what she really wanted — transport twice a week to the Assembly House tea room to be with her friends.

Management can easily make similar mistakes. Users and workers may well know better ways of doing things than do initiators of schemes dreamed up from a distance.

Consultation should not be confused with either democracy or indecisiveness. Consultation means discussing proposals with users and staff, listening to their quibbles and being prepared to change a scheme in the light of what is said, or explaining why the points raised cannot be put into effect. It is too much to expect that everyone will agree with what is proposed — indeed on occasion nobody will! — but everyone is entitled to an explanation as to why their objections cannot be implemented.

We do not intend to discuss techniques of consultation. They will vary according to local circumstances. We wish, however, to stress that consultation is an attitude of mind, and is part of a listening and responding organisation. New legislation has helped to put consultation with users squarely on the agenda — we now have *Access to Client*

Records, *Data Protection Act*, *Complaints Procedure*, the *National Health and Community Care Act*, and the *Children Act* of 1989. What needs to happen is for departments to transfer those same principles to dealing with their own staff.

Failure to do this is meat and drink to the social work press. We are constantly reading about workers objecting to measures hastily put in place without proper consultation. A bit more effort by management to listen to the worries of their staff before taking irrevocable decisions might be the difference between success and failure. At least it might prevent so much time afterwards being spent in internal bickering. We sometimes wonder what the journals would find to write about, if managers managed properly!

Pride

This might seem to be an odd quality to try to develop within the agency, for does not 'pride come before a fall'? But there is a huge difference between arrogance and taking a pride in what you are doing.

We wanted our staff to be proud of being in the social care professions. We wanted them to be proud of being employed by Norfolk County Council. In that way, there was a greater possibility of their taking a pride in carrying out the services which our users required.

But how is this to be done? Social Services, in general, and social work in particular, are notorious for being hammered by the national media. How can anyone feel proud, when being castigated so often?

There is obviously a limit to what one agency can do. But, first and foremost, it is necessary for all staff to feel comfortable and valued in their own setting. If the other aspects mentioned earlier in this chaper are in place, you are largely there already. This should be supplemented by assuring your staff that their job is important and that they are doing it well. And this reassurance should come not only from senior managers but also from those who are ultimately responsible — owners, councillors, chief executives, directors.

But even this is of limited value unless the whole agency is seen to be worthwhile and efficient. It is difficult to feel pride in working for an organisation which is only referred to in derogatory terms. How can this be tackled? May we suggest three ways.

First, make sure that the agency is efficient and quality conscious. Social care agencies are in touch with an awful lot of people, and, if they are satisfied with what you are doing, they will tell other people.

Secondly, take all reasonable opportunities to praise the worthiness of social care — and for those of you working in the public sector, say how proud you are to be doing so. For you should be. Despite the recent propaganda that in some way the public sector is parasitic on the efforts of private enterprise, most of the major improvements to the quality of life (apart from consumer goods and manufacturing) have come from the public sector. And you are part of a very proud tradition!

Thirdly, publicise what you do. Your targets should be your local media, the national social work press, and finally the national media. Not only the good stories — for these will be of limited interest — but take the opportunities presented by difficult problems, locally and nationally. For example, ater the publication of the reports into child deaths and sexual abuse, we offered to explain what went on locally, and were publicised extensively on television, radio and in the press; after the death of an elderly lady in exceptionally squalid circumstances, we received reasonably favourable press and television coverage, because we were prepared to go 'up front' and discuss what had happened. Even when a sexual offender, discharged on licence by the Home Office to one of our hostels, tragically raped a 12 year-old girl, there was a sober debate of the issues involved because we honestly outlined all the problems. Sometimes more appreciation of the work done by social care agencies flows from regrettable incidents than by publicising our 'successes'.

Checklist of main points in Chapter Four

1. The biggest challenge to management is to create the right climate amongst the whole workforce to ensure that what has been planned is actually put into practice.
2. In Norfolk, we found that five aspects need to be addressed in order to establish a positive climate and style: *enthusiasm, imagination, maximisation, consultation* and *pride*.
3. Management needs to eliminate factors which lead to a dispirited workforce:

   - unnecessary change (if it's not bust, don't fix it);
   - staff shortages leading to overwork;
   - inadequate training opportunities;
   - being 'over-controlled';
   - poor accommodation and facilities.

   And then accentuate the positive by setting a leadership style in which the workforce can have confidence, and by ensuring that all members of staff are treated and valued equally.
4. Try to free up the thinking of all staff and encourage them to identify with both problems and the solutions to them. Artificial barriers inhibit imaginative thinking.
5. In order to maximise the use of resources, it is necessary to allow them to be used flexibly.
6. Just as social care workers should consult with service users before deciding on the best way of helping them with their problems, so management needs to listen to its staff before deciding on the most appropriate methods of delivering services.
7. Management should promote an internal and external public relations strategy aimed at making the workforce proud to be employed by them.

5 Aims and values

We will now turn to the analogy set out in Chapter 3 of how a manufacturer would endeavour to produce a car which satisfied his customers. You will recall that the first stage would be to decide what sort of car he was in the business of providing and how he was to build it.

In other words: *vision.* You have to decide exactly what you are intending to provide for potential users of your service, and the principles on which that service delivery will be based. Until the agency does that, you will be uncertain, the staff will be confused and users will be discontented at not knowing what they can truly expect to receive.

This vision should be turned into an unambiguous statement of intent to guide management, workers and users.

To translate this to social care agencies, it is necessary to have a mission statement of your overall aims, together with the principles and values on which the services are to be based. This will be refined further into the precise levels of provision and who would qualify for it — but more of that in the next chapter.

For an example of how this can be done, we would refer you to a Social Services Department of a local authority. The overall Statement of Aims and Values (sometimes called a mission statement) will come from the full Council itself. The Social Services Committee will then produce its own statement based on that already agreed by the Council, and being a committee of the Council, it cannot include things which would be contrary to the overall intention of that body.

The next stage is for each section of the Department to fit its own statement of aims and values into that already agreed for the Department as a whole. Then follow the aims for each particular establishment, and finally — as part of a staff development programme — for each individual.

The whole process cascades downwards, with each subsequent statement adding to, but not detracting from, what went before.

Let us see how this might work in practice.

Aims and values of the organisation or agency

There is no single formula for this statement of intent. In the appendices we give two quite different types. The first — from Wiltshire County Council — is a concise mission statement for all the activities of the County Council, to which would be added subsequently the more specific aims of the Social Services Department. The statement encapsulates in one easily remembered sentence what is the overall aim of the organisation — 'Our business is to listen, respond, serve and excel to make Wiltshire *the* county in which to live and work.' Not quite as catchy as British Telecom's 'It's you we listen to', but just as effective.

The values supporting Wiltshire's statment will come as no surprise to those who have read the preceding chapter — responsiveness to consumers and staff, effective communication, a commitment to quality, a desire for staff to be innovative and enthusiastic, a belief in professional integrity.

The second example comes from Norfolk County Council. It says:

> 'Norfolk County Council exists to serve the people of Norfolk.
>
> 'The Council aims to ensure the provision of the highest possible quality of service within the financial resources available.
>
> 'The Council and its staff will work in an open and accessible manner, treating everyone fairly and with respect.
>
> 'The Council will help and encourage individuals, families, communities and organisations to take responsibility for matters which they can handle satisfactorily themselves.
>
> 'In all its policies, the Council will have regard to the economic well-being of the County, and will be sensitive to the environment and heritage of Norfolk, recognising the contribution they make to the quality of life of local people.'

Obviously, there are differing aims and values amongst local authorities. For example, Norfolk's commitment to equal opportunities is incorporated in the phrase 'treating everyone fairly and with respect': other Councils may choose to make a statement about tackling the causes of discrimination and operating a policy of positive discrimination.

But there is no point in having such a statement unless all staff know about it and are clearly working towards delivering what is contained in it. This brings us to the next stage.

Aims and values of the department

We take as our example how Norfolk Social Services are interpreting the Mission Statement of the County Council. It is contained in 'Statements of Philosophy and Policy for the Provision of Services by Norfolk Social Services Committee', and we have included this in full as an Appendix.

Before commenting on it in detail, let us consider where the ideas came from which are included in it.

It is not difficult to find principles which would gain general acceptance. Department of Health Consultation Papers and Guidelines can form an excellent basis on which local interpretations can be added.

Other examples are available from such documents as the Wagner Report on residential care *A Positive Choice,* which emphasises such factors as the following:

- People who move into a residential establishment should do so by positive choice.
- Living in a residential establishment should be a positive experience ensuring a better quality of life than the resident could enjoy in any other setting.
- Measures need to be taken to ensure that individuals can exercise their rights. Safeguards should be applied when rights are curtailed.
- Residents should have the same right as people living in their own homes to have access to leisure, educational and other facilities offered by the local community and the right to invite and receive relatives and friends as they choose. People who move into a residential establishment should continue to have access to the full range of community support services.

No, the problem is not finding worthy aims to include in the statement of values and principles; it is ensuring that those who own the service and those who work in the agency know what the consequences might be when they put them into effect. The advice of the authors is that, if the aim or principle is not deliverable in the form it is proposed, it needs to be changed.

A quality service cannot be delivered if everyone knows that your aims are unattainable and you are in reality perpetrating a deceit on yourself and your users. If the organisation and culture in the 'Listening Bank' were so rigid that it prevented staff from heeding the individual requests and problems of their customers, then the Mission Statement contained in that motif would become a matter of derision and be a millstone round the necks of staff. For an agency to promulgate an aim or 'vision', it has to be clear that it will put in the effort and resources to make it succeed.

Norfolk Social Services' Philosophical Basis for the Provision of Services might seem odd in that it starts with four 'negatives' in an attempt to define the general limits of what we are trying to do. These 'negatives' are as follows:

- Citizens in any civilised community have a responsibililty to promote their own welfare and that of their family and fellow citizens. The assistance offered by the Department would build on this and not supersede it.
- Services offered by other agencies should be flexible enough to cater for people who have problems in receiving the basic or usual service. The Department therefore would not acquiesce in

the social apartheid of making parallel provision.

- Apart from statutory obligations to protect children and people with a psychiatric illness, the Department accepts that adult citizens have a right to reject offers of assistance, even if this means the continuance of a lifestyle which is disturbing to fellow citizens.
- When we encourage independence and freedom, this means that our service users will be exposed to the same physical and emotional risks as other members of society. We therefore cannot protect our users from every risk.

It was only after setting these limits that we started to identify what the positive aims were and how we hoped to achieve them. But all staff and users need to know what the limits into which the services would be restricted.

And just as the car manufacturer researched the market before designing the car, so it was necessary to consult and debate before the philosophical basis was determined. It is fine to have as an aim 'People should stand on their own feet', but what does that actually mean in practice when you begin to set standards for the service? It is as well to explore this *before* such a statement is included in a statement of aims and values. Where should the boundaries of self-reliance be drawn? In themselves these limits can cause conflict. Everyone — councillor, manager, staff member and user — should know what they mean.

Let us give an example from the first of the four 'negatives':

An elderly man, living alone, receives a weekly visit from his daughter. She has a car and calls at the supermarket for her own groceries. Yet she is refusing to do her father's request to do his weekly shop on the grounds that 'you have paid your rates and taxes all your life, so why shouldn't the State do it?' If there were no other personality problems between the two of them, would you be prepared to refuse him a shopping service on the grounds that it is not unreasonable to expect his daughter to exercise some responsibility? Different authorities would take different decisions. It is important to be clear where your agency stands.

In Norfolk, this limiting factor was debated in public, and the resulting decision was 'owned' by the social services committee, thus giving full backing to departmental staff if a subsequent complaint was received.

This 'ownership' is crucial. If the committee is not prepared to 'sign up' for a policy, principle or aim, it will need to be modified. For example, on page 4 paragraph 5 of the 'Philosophical Basis of Services for Children and Families' (in Appendix 2), you will read: 'the involvement of children and young people in the criminal justice system should be kept to a minimum.' Before that section could be put to committee for approval, seminars were held on the best way of dealing with young offenders, discussions were held with police and magistrates, and papers were debated in public by the committee. Had the councillors not been convinced, and had not the other parties involved been prepared to go along with us, then that underlying principle would not have been promoted.

Aims and principles, when set, are unlikely to change very much, unless there is a radical change of thinking by those who are in charge of the agency — for example, going back to Norfolk's negative limitations, it is possible that public pressure following a number of accidents would insist that, when someone comes into care, all risks and danger be taken from their life, even if this means a curtailment of freedom.

Aims and values of the sections in the department

Incorporated into Norfolk's Philosophy document (see Appendix) are the aims and values for each section of the department. For example, page 4 gives five principles on which services for children and families are to be based:

1. The best interests of the child should be paramount at all times.
2. Children should have a right to a secure and permanent relationship with a familiar group of adults.
3. Children and families should share in the decisions determining their future.
4. Effective services for children and families can only be provided by the community at large and by all appropriate agencies working together.
5. The involvment of children and young people in the criminal justice system should be kept to a minimum.

These principles were approved by the Social Services Committee in 1985 — way before the provisions of the 1989 *Children Act.* And when that Act came into effect, there was no need to change the principles, even though the ways in which they were implemented would have to be modified. (Perhaps this would be an appropriate time to disclaim any particular forethought or knowledge in what Norfolk did. Indeed, those principles — if our memories serve us correctly — we received from a London Borough. We liked them and saw no reason to make any major changes. It is not impossible that the Borough, in its turn, acquired them from another source. In Norfolk we weren't too proud to copy the good things which others had done!)

Aims and values of individual units

Without going into detail, the chain does not stop there. For example, each unit in the children and families section would have their own statement of aims and values. Each children's home would know what it was in the business of providing, and how it would go about the task. So too would the family-finding and adoption unit. But their particular statements would have to fit into the aims and values of the section.

Caveat

You will recall that, early in this chapter, we stressed the importance of being able to deliver whatever aims and values you decide to adopt, and, in fact, of actually delivering them. We would also add the necessity of integrating them into those of other people and agencies with which you will be working to provide a cohesive service.

A particularly poignant reminder of this came to the attention of one of the authors at a national conference of a major voluntary organisation which helps deaf-blind people. Parents were telling of their experiences of finding out that their children had disabilities.

One mother of a 7 year-old boy said that, prior to his birth, she had no idea that her son might have difficulties. But within hours of the delivery, she was spoken to by a paediatrician who asked what she knew about biology. Somewhat puzzled, she replied that she knew probably as much as most people who hadn't specialised in the subject. At which point the paediatrician said: 'I like to give people the information straight. Your son has only half a brain. He has piggy eyes and will never walk. He will not live beyond the age of five. Have you any questions?'

The mother was so stunned that she could not reply. After waiting a few moments, the doctor said: 'Well, I'm rather pushed for time and have to go to the bank.' And, with that, off he went.

But worse was to come. One might have forgiven that brusque approach if there had been someone else assigned to support, counsel and advise. But there wasn't. The nurses knew nothing about the child's condition or the prognosis. No occupational therapist or physiotherapist was called on to give assistance for some considerable time. Social work counselling was totally absent. And when a social worker eventually turned up after many months, she knew nothing about deaf-blindness and offered no counselling about the feelings that the mother and her husband might have at having given birth to a child with such severe disabilities. This latter point is of particular interest. Social workers have been praised for the support and counselling they have given to those who have survived major physical disasters, such as Zeebrugge, Bradford, Hillsborough, King's Cross, Hungerford, Piper Alpha. Many departments have set up specialist teams that can be called together at short notice, if ever a civil disaster occurs in their area. Where is the support and counselling for someone like this mother who had been presented with just as fraught a situation.?

That Social Services Department would no doubt admit that its aims and values would include such things as 'treating an individual with respect', and 'helping people overcome disasters in their life', and 'supporting carers'.

The above example reveals the following factors that should influence a decision as to what should be agreed.

- Before saying, for example, that an aim is 'to give advice and assistance to families to promote the welfare of children and to prevent individuals from becoming in need of care and attention' and implying that this means all children, where is the limit to be drawn?
- If you intend that parents of children with severe disabilities should be offered counselling and guidance as soon as a diagnosis has been made, who is to provide it? In other words, is the task going to be one of *your* agency's aims, or is it going to rest with someone else?
- If you decide that your agency is to deliver a particular service, have you the staff with the knowledge and communication skills to do it? If you have not, do not say that you are going to offer the service.

The setting down of vague but worthy aims and principles is not a very difficult task. Indeed, a vision of where your agency should be going, and what it should be doing, is not too difficult to craft, bearing in mind the wealth of material that is being produced by Government, professional associations, voluntary organisations, public reports and the media. The difficulty lies in ensuring that you confine your objectives — and even your values — into what can be 'owned' by the agency and delivered by it.

One final thought on principles, before we turn to how they can be implemented. To have aims and values which are acceptable to all the agencies providing services for a particular client group is a bonus well worth striving for. The joint planning process is a valuable mechanism, involving as it does health, housing, education, social services, voluntary organisations and — in the more far-seeing areas — the private sector and service users.

More than 10 years ago, one of the authors presented to a Joint Care Planning Group, looking at services for elderly people, a set of principles which included the striving for privacy and the enabling of elderly people to have as much control as possible over their surroundings and the organisation of the services which were being offered to them. The principles were acclaimed and accepted by the whole group. Thereupon, the question could be raised as to how these values were being put into effect in the local hospital, with its long wards and rigid routine. But, once you have done this, expect your own services to be similarly challenged!

Advantages

The above system might seem a bit excessive. Why should you bother? Let us give you a few reasons:

- Members of staff will learn quickly what the organisation is trying to achieve.
- Users will also know what sort of service to expect. (Remember that one of the definitions we gave of quality assurance is 'a system which makes sure that users get what they have been promised.) The statement of aims and values can be said to be some of the promises that are being made.
- If aims and values are written down, they can be challenged.
- Unless you have aims and values, how can you devise standards (see next chapter); if you have unstable standards, how can you monitor and inspect them accurately?

Checklist of main points in Chapter Five

1. The first stage of our quality assurance system is to decide exactly what you are intending to provide for potential users of your service, and the principles on which service delivery will be based. This 'vision' should be turned into an unambiguous statement of intent to guide management, workers and users — a Mission Statement.
2. The aims and values of the agency should be the basis of a statement of aims and values produced by sections, individual units and even individual workers.
3. Aims and values must be achievable and should be congruent with those of other agencies. The joint planning mechanism is a valuable mechanism for attaining this.
4. The advantages of written aims and values are as follows:

   - They ensure that all staff know the direction in which services should be going.
   - Written statements can be more easily challenged and debated than airy-fairy feelings;
   - Service users can know what to expect — and complain if they are not getting it.
   - Without clear aims and values, it is impossible to devise stable standards.

6 Setting the standards

Let us begin with two quotes, both of which come from Department of Health Publications.
The White Paper, *Caring for People*, states in Section 3.4.9:

> It will be essential that, whenever they purchase services, social services authorities should take steps to ensure that the quality to be delivered is clearly specified and properly monitored, bearing in mind that vulnerable people are involved as users.

And on page 23 of *Inspecting for Quality*, we read:

> A standard is a means of judging. Standards are the criteria for judging quality, worth or value. They should be validated.

These put into elegant language the first conclusions that we reached in Norfolk, when we started to inspect our services in 1983 — namely that, if staff do not know explicitly the standards of service they are expected to deliver, they will make up their own, resulting in users receiving differing levels of service from different workers. Moreover, unless standards have been set, neither the agency, the worker nor the user can judge whether a service of the appropriate quality is being provided.

Standards should be based on the aims and values described in the last chapter. They are the measures by which the agency — and the user — can gauge whether the service is successful. In other words, the standards are the promises which the agency gives to the user about the quality of the service that is going to be delivered. For a multitude of reasons, e.g. staff shortages, restrictions on resources, too much work coming in, those promises will vary. Standards, therefore, unlike aims and values, might often be changed for the better or worse according to what it is possible to offer the user. For the credibility of the agency, it is important never to promise the user standards which are impossible to achieve.

Remember one of our definitions of quality assurance is a system which makes sure that service users always get what they have been promised.

Where do standards come from? And who decides which standards are to be set? Let us consider these questions in relation to services for elderly people. We accept that the following statements are something of a caricature, but we hope that they make the point.

From a service user

I want the Social Services Department to help me do the things I now cannot do. I still want to be in control of my life and my activities. I don't want to be a lot of trouble, but I really would like help to be given at a time which is convenient and in the quantity which I feel necessary. Most of all, I would like to be able to choose what happens to me. I now live on my own, and I am lonely and frightened. I would like to go into a residential home, but only if I can choose which one. If they won't pay for me to go into a home, I would like someone to sit with me in the evenings, to keep me company and to chase off those boys who throw stones into my garden. I know that I can still walk well enough to go to the shops, but I am so frightened that I need someone else to do my shopping. I don't want to be a burden to my family, and I don't want my business discussed with the neighbours. Oh, by the way, I don't like my home-help; she won't wash the windows and she is always patronising me — I hate being called 'luv'. My social worker is a bit bossy, but I think she is trying to do her best. I do wish, however, she would get here on time, and not keep me waiting — I keep thinking that something dreadful has happened to her. I wish I had enough money to be on the telephone.

From the social worker

My job is to assess a person's needs, and in my view an elderly person should be encouraged to be as independent as possible for as long as possible. There is a great danger in giving too much help too early, as studies have shown that this can lead to a speedier slump into dependence. Certainly, I believe that admission to residential care can quickly lead to an institutionalised person; an elderly person may not realise this when they ask to go into a home. There are times therefore when I have to provide services which may not be what the elderly person might choose, but which I am convinced are in their best interests. Wherever possible I try to involve family, neighbours and voluntary groups in a network of care. I need clear direction from my managers about the sort of referrals I can leave alone. I am getting so many elderly people passed on to me by housing departments and health authorities that I am frightened I will end up being criticised personally in the coroners' court. It is alright for hospitals to cut back their waiting lists by keeping people in hospital for shorter periods, but how am I supposed to cope with the increased workload? Oh, and I do wish that I could be trusted to make my own decisions, rather than having to refer any request for a resource to my seniors.

From the local politician (in power!)

My bottom line is that I don't want any tragedy to occur which would reflect badly on the Council. And for the sake of my constituents, I have to watch the pennies. Our community charge is already so high that it is imperative that all expenditure is contained to within the budget that has been set. We spend almost half our social services budget on old people, so I am quite confident that enough money is available to make sure that all the most needy cases are dealt with, providing departmental management efficiently sorts out priorities and controls expenditure. Money must be targeted to those in greatest need. Consumer choice can only be allowed if there is the money to pay for it. Anyone seeking help from the Council — especially elderly people — should be dealt with promptly and in a way that they understand; I expect letters to be answered by return, in language that people can understand, phone calls to be returned and all users to be dealt with courteously. The image of the Council is at stake.

From a carer

Oh for a single comprehensive source of information! I get bits and pieces from all over the place, but I am sure that I still don't know everything that I should. I love my mother but at times she drives me round the bend, especially when my children come home from school and my husband returns from work. Why on earth cannot my mother have day-care in the evenings and at weekends, so that the rest of the family can have a semblance of a normal life without her hanging round our necks all the time? It is unfair for social services to leave so much of my mother's care to me, because it's affecting my family. I won't put her in a home permanently because that would kill her, but I would like some more relief during school holidays. A bit of home-care in the mornings and evenings would be useful, and someone to 'mother-sit' occasionally so that we can go down to meet our friends in the pub.

From the man or woman in the street and the media

There should be somewhere to put old people when they can't look after themselves any more. It is not right that they should live in dirty conditions or wander the streets without proper clothes on. Social services are too wishy-washy. Everybody knows that sometimes old people can't be held responsible for their actions; they then have to be protected. And look at that case last week when that old man from that old people's home was killed crossing the road: he should have been locked in. He wasn't being looked after properly. Heads should roll.

From the health authority

Our job is to help sick people get better. It is not to provide social care, when social services cannot organise it. We are under pressure ourselves. There is the usual shortage of money, and we are also being criticised for our long waiting lists. We can shorten those lists by reducing the time people stay in hospital. We want quicker responses from social services, and greater amounts of care in the home. If they cannot deliver this, our only option is to arrange for people to go into private homes. What happens after that is between them and social services. Moreover, we hear from consultants that, sometimes, general practitioners are applying for their patients to be admitted to hospital largely for medical conditions that could be dealt with at home but there was no one available to care for the patients. That, in our view, should be the task of the local authority to provide, not us.

From the voluntary organisation

We are here to fill in the gaps left by the statutory agencies, not to be the main source of support to vulnerable elderly people. We believe that we are being abused by those agencies because of our willingness to help. But they are passing over to us responsibilities that our volunteers are not trained to accept, and when we ask for funds to employ professionals, we are refused. Our volunteers just cannot cope with the confused people who are now being referred to us.

From minority groups

No one seems to know how to provide care which is acceptable to the older people in our community. We need those who run the services to listen to what we are saying, and as a very minimum we want those who offer help to be able to communicate with us. Perhaps the best way of providing services would be for us to do it ourselves, but they won't give us the money. They just don't understand.

From the private home owner

We believe in choice. If an old person wants to come into a home, they should be enabled to do so. Those who haven't the money should be paid for by the state.

And so on, and so on. We haven't mentioned the directions and advice emanating from government, from national organisations and from inquiries — or even the poor Director of Social Services, who is expected by all the above to agree with everybody's points of view!

So, who has the responsibility for determining those standards?

Although there are so many people who have an interest in the levels of service which are to be delivered, the final say must rest with those who are responsible for the agency itself and its functioning. In other words, it is the Council (through its councillors) or the owner of an home who determines the level. We have often heard staff — especially social workers — say that they are accountable to their clients. This is a nice idea, but in the real world a worker is accountable to the people who employ them to do a particular job, and the task they do has to be satisfactory to those footing the bill. If it is not, you will no doubt be looking for another sponsor!

So, it is the Council or the home owner who will agree on the standards that are to be applied. But before that, it would be wise for there to be a process of consultation. You would be foolish to assume that interested parties in your own areas have the same stereotyped views as those mentioned above. In particular, close consultation with the staff who are to put the standards into effect will ensure that what is being demanded can actually be delivered — and, of course, the users, but more of that in Chapter 9.

Setting standards for a social care agency is not easy. Indeed, the art is so much in its infancy, it may be better to think in terms of standards evolving rather than being set once and for all. One of the lessons learned from Norfolk's first forays into inspections back in 1983 was that, as a result of the inspection, it was sometimes necessary to rethink the standards against which the inspections were being made. The standards fondly set in isolation by management and committee were just not realistic or were too confusing for the staff.

In our view there are three areas of activity for which standards can be set — consumer care, operational targets, and the inputs which would be necessary in order for those targets to be achieved. As we discuss them in more detail, it will become clear that, although the Council or owner has to take ultimate responsibility for the levels of service, a wise Council will delegate the setting of certain of these standards to its professional staff.

Consumer care standards

These are basically how the organisation sets out to deal with the users of its services. The image of an American receptionist with a fixed smile on her face urging everyone 'to have a nice day' is a crude example.

If we examined the work of an area of social workers, the areas covered by the term 'consumer care' would include how callers to the office are received, appointment systems, response times to requests for help, replying to letters, returning telephone calls, keeping to appointment times, the physical conditions where callers are received and interviewed, informing referrers about the results of your action, the ability to receive requests for help from people whose spoken English is poor. The list is almost endless. It could also include such things as how staff should be dressed, and incorporate values such as honesty, integrity, cheerfulness, concern, respect, treating people as individuals.

The standards would define the minimum level of functioning for the agency to feel it was successfully attaining its objectives. They would be pitched at a level that was achievable. Through the training of staff and their familiarity with the required practice, the agency would be trying constantly to improve on that minimum standard. Indeed, a good organisation would be constantly urging its workers to find better ways of doing things, and the best organisations would find ways of rewarding those staff who can point to improvements.

To give a few examples of consumer care standards, which should be common enough to raise no eyebrows:

- Waiting areas will be cleaned twice each day, and be furnished with a range of different types of chair and have an up-to-date copy of the local paper available.
- A reply will be sent to all incoming correspondence within 5 working days. If — on the day of receipt — it is estimated that a full reply will take longer, then an immediate acknowledgement will be sent, which will indicate when a reply can be expected.
- All letters will state clearly the name of the person dealing with the matter.
- When going out of the office, staff should leave a message for the telephonist as to where they are going and when they next might be available.
- Staff should not wear clothing which might lead users to believe that they are not being dealt with by someone from a professional organisation.
- When a telephone call is put through to an extension, no caller should be left holding on the telephone for more than 30 seconds.

These standards apply to all staff — indeed, they could apply across all Council departments. They can be set by councillors, once they have been advised whether they are achievable or what the resource implications might be.

When we come to monitoring and inspection, it would not be difficult to reach a judgement as to whether the standards are being achieved.

Standards for operational outputs

'Outputs' are descriptions of what is to be produced or achieved in order to achieve the outcomes or aims you have set yourself (and which were discussed in the last chapter).

Let us take, as an example, the outcome (or aim) — childen should have a right to a secure and permanent relationship with a familiar group of adults. One of the operational standards that could be set is that no child should remain in residential care for more than 6 months. If that standard is reached, the original aim is fulfilled.

Another example from the field of childcare could be that to encourage parents to accept responsibility for their children — if this is one of your aims — no child committed to the care of the Authority should remain 'home on trial' or 'home in care' for more than 3 months without the order being revoked. (May we make it clear that we are not suggesting these targets are the best that can be set, only that they would exemplify what we are discussing!)

Similarly, for elderly people, you might set yourself an outcome that elderly people should be enabled to lead as independent a life as possible. One output which could help to achieve this is to agree that anyone medically fit for discharge, but who required social care, would be discharged within 3 working days of the Department being notified.

Perhaps one of your outcomes is that elderly people in residential care should have their dignity and freedom of choice preserved. What standards of output would be set?

Presumably, they would be the same as we ourselves would expect from our holiday hotel — choice of menu and flexible meal-times, clean tablecloths and cutlery. Most of us would prefer to serve ourselves from tureens and would like access to drink-making facilities either in our rooms or close by.

Few of us would like to share rooms with strangers, and we would like *en suite* facilities. Any toilets for general use must be clean and have locks on the doors.

These are just a few examples. It is not too difficult to come up with standards for almost anything, if you ask the people who are at the receiving end. As we said earlier, a far more difficult task is deciding what is possible to be delivered.

These standards should receive the detailed approval of the Social Services Committee. Not only would the Committee have to accept that these targets typified the sort of service they intended to be delivered, but they would have to be convinced by professional management that they should be, and could be, achieved. And, as so many of the outcomes require the co-operation of other agencies, they would also have to be assured by their senior managers that the relevant discussions and negotiations had been completed successfully.

Standards of inputs and processes necessary to achieve operational outcomes

These are probably the most difficult to define, not because no one knows how to do it but because a balance has to be struck between putting professional staff into operational strait-jackets and encouraging them to use their knowledge and intelligence to find innovative and flexible ways of achieving the targets that have been set for them.

But we are convinced that there are ways of doing this. If we return to the operational target that no child should remain in residential care for longer than 6 months, there are actions which could help to achieve that target, and with which the agency legitimately could expect all its professional staff to comply. The following are examples:

- Each child admitted to residential care will, within 1 month of being admitted, have their needs assessed and a preliminary care plan determined.
- A fostering officer will attend such reviews, and in the event of the placement in care being estimated as likely to exceed 6 months, will begin steps to secure a suitable placement.
- If the care plan indicates that the child should return to his/her natural family, a contract will be drawn up between all parties indicating the things that will have to be done and the timescale.
- Within a further 2 months a full review of progress will be held. Organisational factors which might be hampering the implementation of the care plan should be referred to the team manager.

This basic framework of standards of procedure should help the professional to fulfil the operational target, and should, at the same time, reassure the agency that proper steps are being taken. The professional worker is not instructed as to whether the child returns home or is placed in a foster-home. Nor is there direction as to the best plan for child and family. That is left to professional judgement. But the agency has clearly spelled out the essential steps and time-frame within which those professional decisions are to be taken.

One of the authors recently gave this example in the NALGO/JICC Distance learning material.

> 'We might have set a standard for the output of allowing elderly people control over the menu and times of eating along the following lines:
>
> - A cooked breakfast to the choice of the resident will be available between the hours of 8 am and 9.30 am. A continental breakfast or cereals can be had in the dining room between 7 am and 11 am.

- As there is not the staffing to produce a cooked meal both at lunch-time and in the evening, the majority of residents have chosen to have the main hot meal at 12.30 pm. There will be a choice of two meat dishes and a vegetarian meal. Each month a survey will be carried out into the kinds of dishes residents would prefer.
- Tea will be a cold buffet meal and will be available in the dining room any time from 4.30 pm to 7.00 pm.

If that is the output you wish to have, you must then ask what you have to do in order to achieve it. A procedure will have to be drawn up on such things as how surveys are to be carried out, how food is to be ordered and stored, whether residents are to be supervised during the whole of the extended meal times. This procedure can be said to be setting the standards for the process.'

Standards for inputs also cover the abilities of staff. It would be quite legitimate for the agency to set a standard of training and competences without which staff would not be able to do certain kinds of work. The Mental Health Act does this by precluding anyone without Approved Social Worker Approval from assessing whether someone should be admitted to hospital under the Act. Other examples would be in relation to child abuse or child sexual abuse; no one could investigate or become a key worker in such cases without undergoing specialised training. Or what about working with ethnic minority communities? The agency could specify the knowledge and training of staff who may be asked for assistance. And don't forget support staff. They too have competences.

A final thought on inputs — it is even possible to set standards for a quality assurance system. For example, Norfolk has determined that the overall quality standards to be achieved are:

- to offer a customer-oriented service;
- to offer a prompt and appropriate response to customers' requests;
- to satisfy the individual needs of customers most appropriately by involving them in the decision-making process;
- to use resources effectively and imaginatively for the benefit of customers.

So far, we have only discussed possible standards set by committee or senior management. Just as with aims and values, standards can also be set by sections and units within the overall framework of departmental and agency directions. It is right that the aims and major operational targets for each home, day centre and section is set by the agency, so that comprehensive cover for users can be assured. But, within those, the staff within each unit could, with benefit, determine what standards and targets the unit and its workers have to reach in order for the overall objectives to be reached. This analysis would not only help staff to understand and 'own' the standards set by senior management, but would also involve the interest and commitment to achieve self-appointed tasks and targets. And a detailed review, unit by unit, of the skills they require to maintain the standards set for them will be the basis of a staff development and training programme.

Setting standards may not be easy. They may even be said by some to be unnecessary 'because professional workers know what they are doing'. But, in our view, the long and sometimes tedious process in identifying them is valuable for a variety of reasons.

- Thinking about them clarifies exactly what the agency is about and how it would like its services delivered.
- It should ensure that problems are only tackled by staff with the proper competences.
- The setting of standards is a marvellous opportunity for management to consult with those who deliver and receive the services.
- Unless you have identified standards, how do you (or anyone else) know whether or not you are doing a good job. This latter point is becoming more important for agencies, as dissatisfied users are turning to courts for compensation. The fact that an agency has defined standards, and a system for delivering them, can be a good protection.

Perhaps this is the time for us to consider the International Standard for quality assurance ISO 9000 and British Standard BS 5750 (part 2), which interprets it for social care agencies. ISO 9000 was originally produced as the standard for industrial organisations, but the system it describes can be translated into a system suitable for social care agencies. This interpretation has been done by British Quality Association's Social Care Sector Committee. We are indebted to Clive Bone, the Chair of the Local Authority Sector Committee, for the following synopsis of ISO 9000.

> This Standard comprises those things that good organisations ought to be addressing. It is basically a code of sound management practice and should be seen as such. Its language, however, reflects its industrial origins and it tends to be inpenetrable at the first reading. The organisational factors covered by the Standard address the following issues:
>
> - ***Organisation and responsibilities***
>
> Quality policy should be known and clearly stated. This should reflect the customer's needs and expectations, the market situation, the requirements of society — the laws, the environment, etc — and the policy should be the drivng force behind quality management. Clarity of organisation and responsibilities within the organisation is a key issue, and the guidance in the Standard in relation to policy places considerable weight on the customer's needs.

- ***Written procedures***

ISO 9000 demands the documentation of key procedures, and the adequate control of documentation, i.e. how it is issued and updated. There is logic in this. It forces you to think about what you do and set it down in writing. Writing things down — whilst addressing the operational demands of ISO 9000 at the same time — will unearth unresolved problems that will have to be faced.

- ***Verification***

The Standard contains criteria for inspection and verification by the supplying organisation. This is, of course, quality control, but the procedures are built into the working regime and may not result in the employment of 'inspectors' as such.

- ***Records***

An adequate system of records is necessary to review progress and improve quality — management information upon which to base better procedures. Quality demands an informed, proactive approach and such records would include purchasing records — the performance and value of bought out goods — and inspection reports.

- ***Audit***

A system based on ISO 9000 can be audited, just as can a financial system. The audits can be both internal and external — and it is this that ensures that the system is being maintained.

Clive Bone comments:

It must be stressed that organisations should never think in terms of 'working to' ISO 9000. The key lies in developing existing procedures and practices such as they are in accordance with ISO 9000. In other words, use ISO 9000 as a basic yardstick to measure how you manage. Nor is ISO 9000 exhaustive; some industrial organisations use superior systems of their own — Ford Motors, for example. Nevertheless, it provides a disciplined framework for quality management, and one would hope that local authorities would want to have systems at least equal to ISO 9000 as a matter of policy.

In reality much of ISO 9000 is applied common sense, and, to encourage its adoption, the Government established the National Accreditation Council for Certification Bodies (NACCB), a body whose task is to 'accredit' the bodies who audit the quality management systems of suppliers and certify them accordingly. To encourage this further, there are grants to assist smaller firms to achieve 'quality certification', and these grants currently cost the taxpayer some £12 million per year.

We have quoted Clive at length, because his work with the British Quality Association has helped him to become one of the foremost authorities on quality assurance throughout Europe.

We therefore commend to you ISO 9000 and its translation to social care agencies, BS 5750 — and we do so not only because one of the authors of this book was the Chair of the Committee which produced the interpretation! For further information and copies of BS 5750, we suggest you contact the British Quality Association, 10 Grosvenor Gardens, London SW1W 0DQ.

It was encouraging to read in *Care Weekly* on 1.11.91 that Napier House (a home for eldery people run by Newcastle Social Services) is the first residential care home in England to be a holder of the British Standard BS 5750. May there be many more!

We have diverted somewhat from the original theme of this chapter, which was the setting of standards. We have already discussed the importance of determining the standards to which everyone in the agency should be working, but a word of warning. It may be too extravagant to claim that standards cannot make good workers, and that all they do is to help eliminate the poorest practice. But that is not far from the mark.

Staff cannot consistantly do good work for the agency without there being clear standards to which they can work, and yet clear standards in themselves cannot make a bad worker good. Do you remember the experiences of Admiral Rickover described in Chapter 1? Standards are only part of a framework in which good practice can flourish. Remember, standards define the minimum level below which the agency must not fall if it is to meet the aims and values it has set for itself. The culture of your organisation should be such that staff are striving to do better than that minimum. Standards are the baseline for improvement; they are not targets to be worked down to.

It almost goes without saying that the standards will be largely ineffective unless they are 'owned' by a workforce that wants to implement them. Threats of disciplinary action rarely achieve enthusiasm and innovation. But more of that in the next chapter.

To sum up the importance of standards we quote from the submission made by Norfolk Social Services when applying for The British Quality Award Scheme for 1991.

> The key elements of our quality assurance system are the same as for other industries.
>
> - Standards must be set. These standards should be the minimum acceptable standard. If the service falls below this level, it is not thought that the needs of our customers are being met satisfactorily. The service provided frequently will be above this level, and this, of course, is to be encouraged. However, the standards set must be accepted and respected, and must be realistically attainable.
> - The standards must be recognised throughout the organisation. Everyone must be involved in setting, and achieving, their own standards in their own particular field.
> - Achieving these standards must be adopted as an integral part of the day-to-day activities of everyone involved in the organisation. Quality can only be built in by the people who are doing the job themselves.
> - The scheme must be customer centred, which means that all decisions must be seen in relation to the impact on customers.
>
> The process need to be co-ordinated to make sure that each individual effort is made to support the overall aims of the organisation. To make sure that this happens, staff must be given information and guidance, as well as opportunities to develop their skills.

Checklist of main points in Chapter Six

1. Unless standards have been set, neither the agency, the worker nor the user can judge whether a service of the appropriate quality is being provided.
2. Standards should be based on the statement of aims and values. They are the 'promises' which the agency gives to the user about the quality of service that is going to be delivered.
3. For the credibility of the agency, it is important never to promise standards which cannot be achieved. Standards, therefore, may have to be changed in the light of the agency's ability to deliver.
4. Standards are set by those who control the agency, but, before setting them, they should take into account, the opinions of users, workers, other agencies and public opinion.
5. Standards define the lowest (not the maximum!) level below which an agency cannot fall if it is to meet the aims and values it has set for itself.
6. There are three areas of activity for which standards can be set:

   - Consumer care, in other words how the agency sets out to deal with the users of the service.
   - Standards for Operational Outputs, i.e. what is to be produced or achieved in order to reach the outcomes or aims which you have set for yourself.
   - Standards of inputs and processes necessary to achieve operational outcomes.

7. British Standard BS 5750 (Part 2) can be used to interpret quality assurance for social care agencies.
8. Standards will be largely ineffective unless they are 'owned' by a workforce which wants to implement them.

7 Setting up the assembly line

Assembly line is a funny phrase to use, isn't it? Indeed, on occasions when we have lectured on this subject, some of the audience has reacted strongly against it. They picture men and women in overalls wielding welding irons, or packing things into boxes. Surely the delivery of social care cannot be compared to such a restricted and mind-numbing process?

But, if we rid ourselves of the pictorial constraints of this type of routine activity, many of the underlying principles for achieving quality are the same.

In the first place, we should realise that no one in a social care agency works totally in isolation. Rarely is the service given solely by one person, and, even if it is, then that person will be helped and supported by a range of other people — clerks, finance officers, supervisors, managers. And, if any of the supporting staff do not function adequately, then the capacity of the front-line worker will be diminished. All have to do their bit in sequence before a quality service can be guaranteed.

Perhaps the metaphor is more acceptable if ever we consider the concepts behind care assessment, care management and service provision. Here, there is a clear picture of one person doing their own part of the process, perhaps having received part of the package from someone else and perhaps passing on their own work for someone else to take it forward.

Be that as it may, the points that we are initially trying to make are:

- the necessity for each person in the process knowing exactly how their part of the work fits into the whole;
- how each person relies on other people to do their own job properly;
- the importance of knowing how one person's activities affect the performance of others.

The whole organisation cannot pull together towards a common purpose if various workers operate in closed boxes and could not care less if that affected their colleagues.

It is not uncommon for there to be regular team meetings of peer workers. But do all members of a chain or assembly line meet — especially if they work in different departments? So often we have heard complaints about professional staff not bothering to collect the information necessary for the administrative or finance officer to do their job, or professional staff whingeing about the unwillingness of the clerks to 'be helpful'. And what of other departments? Merely to send and receive stroppy memos from the Treasurer or Personnel Officer does little to build up the atmosphere and climate in which a quality service can be given. Even if we accept that it is the role of managers to ensure that all activities are properly interlinked, it is valuable for front-line staff to meet from time to time with the colleagues from other sections or departments on whom they rely. Understanding each others' jobs, and what might create difficulties, would be a first step in deleting some of the negative factors which hinder the 'seamless' service.

There are lessons in this chapter which could be applied to the relationship between local authorities and the independent residential care sector. Although inspection units can take a snapshot twice per year of what is going on in a residential care home, is this the prime way to ensure high-quality standards? Inspection does little except praise the good and point out what is wrong. It doesn't actually promote quality positively. If independent proprietors understood the ingredients of a quality assurance system and were willing to put them into effect in their own establishments, the chances of a permanent quality service would be increased.

We believe that, if local authorities spent as much time encouraging and assisting home owners to have an efficient 'assembly line' as they do carrying out sporadic inspections, the quality of care in the independent sector would benefit. But perhaps local authorities have enough to do initially in ensuring the quality of their own operations.

Instruction and direction

It may seem axiomatic that workers will not provide the service required of them by their managers — and the service users — if they do not know what they are supposed to be doing. But it is one thing for management to promulgate a policy; it is another to do it in such a way that staff understand it and can act on it. For heavy procedure manuals to thud down on the workers' desk does not mean that they will be read!

Before producing any procedures, the agency has to decide how much to concentrate on outcomes and allowing staff the maximum freedom to use their own initiative, or whether workers should have detailed instructions to do things in exactly the same way in the hope that this will lead to a similar result each time. Much will depend on the culture of the organisation and the training given to staff, but our view is that over-concentration on processes will lead staff to consider these to be ends in themselves. *Guides to good practice* defining the aims, values and standards for a service — supported by detailed administrative procedures — may be preferable.

The way in which many Departments have responded so positively to the *Children Act* 1989 is to be applauded and should be copied. Thanks to funding from the Department of Health, staff of all functions and grades are invited to training sessions, which not only set out the changes in the law but also give people the opportunity to discuss, argue and absorb.

Internalising the intention and the desired outcome may be more valuable than learning a detailed procedure. Indeed, the 'why' is as important for a quality service as the 'how'. For, as we have said over and over again, quality will only be delivered if it is 'owned' by the workforce.

Obviously, it would be excessive for there to be such intensive training whenever a new policy document was issued by managers, but, as a minimum, space should be found on the agenda of all management and team meetings whereby new instructions could be explained and understood.

Procedures will be better absorbed by staff, if:

- consultations take place beforehand with staff. Let each procedure come out first in draft. Only foolish managers have the arrogance to believe that they know all the consequences of their actions. It is not a sign of weakness to seek the views of people who will be expected to carry out the order. Getting things right is one of the prerequisites of a quality service;
- they are written in a form and in language which staff can understand easily. If you have difficulty in writing simple language, why not seek the assistance of the authority's press officer?
- they are put on computer in order to overcome the perennial problem of updating — providing staff have access to a terminal;
- each procedure has a summary check-list of action to be taken. Many procedures are long-winded and full of lengthy explanations. Whereas it is helpful for staff to understand the reasons behind the action, a checklist of main points should be produced, to which workers can easily refer and possibly carry around with them;
- dates for implementation are scheduled to enable staff maximum chance to absorb the changes. (Please bear in mind when you are introducing your new system of quality assurance!)

Of particular importance in any procedure is what is to be done if the instructions cannot be carried out, or if the preferred course of action is impossible, perhaps because of a lack of suitable resources. Sometimes this can be incorporated into the procedure itself, for example, assigning priorities to work and giving absolution to staff whose workload does not allow them to deal with referrals of the lowest categories of need. At other times, there will be instructions to whom the staff member should turn for resolution of the problem. At the very least, staff should know what they are to tell potential users if they cannot deliver.

In the next chapter of this book, we will address the issues of monitoring and inspection. One of the aspects to be covered will be the relevance and understandability of the instructions to which staff are supposed to be working. Procedures — like services — should be evaluated from the standpoint of those receiving them as well as those producing them. One thing discovered by the authors when inspecting services, is that, if instructions are unclear from the point of view of those receiving them, they will do their own thing and make up their own!

One further thought on direction. Many Departments are in the throes of restructuring for a plethora of reasons, one of the commonest being the desire to split assessment of need from provision of services. We have heard from the staffs of so many agencies that, with all the other problems they are facing, they see little value in further disruption for what they see to be purely theoretical or political reasons. The remarks made above about the need for consultation are probably even more necessary in respect of a restructuring which changes the basis on which many workers deliver their skills. Many staff simply do not see the advantage of creating artificial barriers when one of the pillars for a quality service is encouraging workers of all kinds to co-operate fully and to use their initiative and flexibility. Before embarking on such a potentially divisive adventure, we advise that you take enough time and trouble to win the hearts and minds of your staff. If they do not 'own' the thinking behind the changes, cynicism will soon set in. And cynicism is the enemy of quality.

Training/staff development

In addition to the usual reason for training (i.e. it is no good just telling people what to do, if they haven't the skill and understanding with which to carry out the instruction), may we advance another. In a labour-intensive organisation such as a social care agency, human resources are amongst its most important assets. Training/staff development can release the potential hiding in these resources.

You will remember in Chapter 4 we discussed the importance of creating the right climate for quality to grow and develop. We suggested that staff should be encouraged not only to use their initiative in seeking solutions to the problems posed by service users, but also to maximise whatever resources are at their disposal. But staff can only align their enthusiastic responses to the requirements of service user and agency if they have the confidence of a sound knowledge base.

The main function of training, however, must be to ensure that each person on the assembly line has the skills necessary to do their particular job. This is a necessity, not a luxury. The authors have great difficulty in thinking of any quality service or product that has to rely on operatives unsure of what they are doing. As we have said before: 'Inspection by itself will not ensure quality; what is required is a committed and knowledgeable workforce responding to the needs of individual service users.'

Of course, the better skilled the workforce, the less time and effort has to be spent on checking up on what they are doing. But more of this in the next chapter.

Perhaps we should define our terms. We use training to mean a planned process to modify attitude, knowledge or skill to achieve effective performance of an activity or range of activities. Development is the realisation of a person's ability or potential. Both are required if the agency is to unlock the skills of its workforce.

For over 10 years Norfolk has been committed to post-qualifying training for professional staff. A Diploma in Management for the Caring Professions (PQS Standard) has been developed in conjunction with Nottingham Polytechnic. We are delighted that all senior departmental managers have attended this course and its predecessor. In the last intake, we were joined by three participants from the private sector. A PQS on Mental Health has been set up in conjunction with Surrey University and the Regional Health Authority, to which health colleagues were invited as well as social workers.

More recently, a Consortium of East Anglian agencies has already set up PQS courses on Services for Elderly People and on Services for Children and Families, both of which have had their second intake of students. The same consortium, including the Regional Health Authority with support from Norwich City College, is pushing forward a plan to develop a further course on Services for People with Learning Difficulties.

Such PQS activity does, however, impinge on a very small percentage of the workforce of most social care agencies — probably less than 10 per cent. And whereas it is right that users with the most complex of problems can have confidence that there is someone in the organisation with the specialist knowledge to help them, there is a great danger that management will concentrate a disproportionate amount of their resources on comparatively few people.

Having the skill and knowledge to do their particular job is a pre-requisite for *all* staff. A quality service will not be given if large sections of the workforce are offered access to minimal training opportunities.

It is not one of the objectives of this book to set out, in any detail, the training opportunities which nationally and locally are now available. To describe and interpret the new system of National Vocational

Qualifications, and to discuss how best they can be introduced into a large organisation would be a book in itself! Suffice it to say that NVQ is competence based and employer led; it has the added advantage of developing skills which are interchangeable between various agencies, an important asset with the progressive blurring between health care and social care. In our view, it is in the interests of employers, staff and users to make this new system work.

Training and staff development are far too important to be left solely to a training sections and consortia! The lead must come from the top management, not only in promoting a culture within the agency which values the contribution to be made by training, but also to decide on priorities — having seen the results of inspections.

Staff development is one of the prime functions of line managers. We are delighted to see the shift in supervision sessions away from checking on what has happened. Instead, supervisors are looking at factors which are hampering an efficient delivery of service as well as how to develop the skills of their staff.

There are many ways of learning apart from formal college courses. Learning from experienced colleagues is still one of the most effective ways of developing skills, and we are delighted that some of the thinking going into post-qualifying and advanced qualifications now recognise this. Specific discussions through a supervision session are one way of imparting knowledge and ideas. Guided discussions amongst colleagues or in staff meetings are another. We often hear criticisms that staff meetings are a waste of time, and no doubt some are. But, if there is a clear agenda, focused discussions, and a time limit put on them, they can be a most effective way of consulting, motivating and training staff.

Norfolk Social Services has set the following goals:

- Each member of staff will have a statement of the framework of training mutually agreed as appropriate for their development. This will include induction, basic training, top-up courses and post-qualification training.
- Training will be client-centred.
- Training will also be made available for all appropriate staff on finance, recruitment, health and safety and the handling of disciplinary matters.
- Management training will be provided for all staff who have management responsibilities and for those who have the potential to become managers.
- Appropriate specialist training will be provided, e.g. child abuse, approved social worker course on mental health, old-age abuse, Alzheimer's disease, AIDS and HIV, race relations and equal opportunities, etc.
- Staff will be encouraged to attend relevant outside courses and conferences. They will be expected to provide written reports

which will enable the benefits of their attendance to be circulated around the Department.

Pie in the sky? We think not, although we accept that, when money is tight, to hold on to the training budget (or even increase) is difficult. We wonder if Toyota has cut back on training its staff during the present recession? We suspect that they restricted the width of their activities rather than the quality! Often Councillors do not appreciate the value of the time spent giving staff the necessary skills, and will consider reducing the staff development and training budget. And yet many of them (from all parties) in their own working lives have undergone apprenticeships and professional training, and, if asked directly, would not settle for a second-rate service for their constituents given by under-skilled staff. Thank goodness the Department of Health recognises the problem and has encouragingly made specific training grants available to local authorities.

Time, space and equipment

Even with the best instruction and training, quality work will not be produced by workers who do not have enough time to do a proper job or who have inadequate working conditions and equipment. One would hardly expect a car of quality to be produced: if a worker on the assembly line had a welding torch that kept breaking down, if he kept tripping over the feet of the next worker, and if suddenly his workload increased by 25 per cent because one of the other workers was off sick.

We hope that the above description does not ring too many bells with you! But it does happen in social care agencies, doesn't it? Offices have too few telephone lines, computers keep breaking down, mileages are cut so that staff cannot use their cars. Offices are cramped, noisy and sometimes dirty. As far as we are aware, local authorities do not expect their Chief Executives and Directors of Social Services to work without easy access to a phone or in surroundings where there can be no quiet or privacy. If the efficiency of the Chief Officer is enhanced by good working conditions, why not that of the workers as well?

And what happens when there are staff vacancies? Because of a general restriction on expenditure — and sometimes because of community charge capping — decisions are taken to slow down recruitment or even to freeze posts when they become vacant. In exceptional cases, staff are encouraged to leave through early retirement schemes, and then are not replaced. To make things worse, little account is taken of the extra demands being made on the service by users, when their expectations have been rightly roused by the information now readily available about what local authorities are legally obliged to provide.

What price quality in such circumstances?

It is interesting to speculate what would happen, when the disgruntled service user turns to the complaints procedure now available. Would the finger of blame be levelled against the overstretched worker? Or against management who have given inadequate directions on priorities? Or against the councillors who have failed to face up to saying which work will no longer be done?

We firmly believe that, whenever there is an acknowledged shortfall in personnel or resources, the 'width' of an agency's activites sometimes has to be reduced in order to ensure that minimum 'quality' standards can be met. And potential service users need to be told if they are no longer going to receive a service so that they have an opportuity of seeking other solutions to their problems. Failure to do this could otherwise lead to:

- potential service users being confined dishonestly to the limbo of an ever-increasing waiting list, hoping for a service which the agency knows that it will never deliver;
- demoralised and overstretched staff being bombarded with complaints from people put on that waiting list, and not being able to do anything about it;
- mistakes being made, which are not only uncomfortable or dangerous to the user but are an inefficient use of time to have to rectify. They may even lead to claims for compensation;
- remaining staff 'voting with their feet', thus exacerbating the situation;
- the potential for industrial action, where management may lose control over which work needs to be done, or even where users receive no service at all. The unedifying spectacle of staff leaving case-files on the Director's desk hardly engenders a spirit of quality!

If managers and councillors fudge this issue, the outcome is likely to be low morale, staff sickness, poor job performance and poor-quality work. Although councillors might dislike telling their constituents that the expected service can no longer be delivered, the consequences of not doing so are potentially far more damaging to user, staff and to themselves politically.

So, what is to be done?

We suggest a workload management system, which will ensure that staff are not given more work than they can cope with. Time was, when some managers were reluctant to introduce a mechanism which gave information and therefore power to their workers. For, when a member of staff had a full measured workload, he could, with justification, refuse to accept any more, thus creating problems for the manager. But properly worked out, the system can, in fact, help the manager, and protect everyone from the horrors of mistakes. It would probably also lead to more work being done; for it is an irony that, the more overworked a person is, the less they actually do. They can spend so much time and thought into worrying about what they are not doing properly that they end up doing less than normal!

Without going into details (for there are many successful systems of workload management), we believe that the skeleton should consist of the following which was pioneered by George Gawlinski, Senior District Manager in West Norfolk:

1. Set aims and objectives for the team.
2. Create a statement of priorities, i.e. the work that *must* be done, or work which is desirable but not essential, and work that will not be done when under pressure.
3. Clarify individual roles and accountabilities, and set key tasks and targets, giving time-budgets for each.
4. Draw up individual and team workload budgets in three areas: maintenance (e.g. team meetings, admin., duty, consultation); casework/case-related activity (i.e. an estimate of the total time available to client groups), and additional work tasks (e.g. attendance in court, working parties, student supervision, committee meetings).
5. Each month, manager and social worker will review the workload. During the review each will look at diary and time logs and take stock of where the time is going. They will assess the stresses and gaps, adjust priorities as necessary, move cases and redefine gate-keeping.
6. Twice a year, the whole team will review whether objectives are being met and quality standards are being maintained. When appropriate, standards will be redefined and tasks redistributed.

This workload management system emphasises the value of regular diarying/monitoring of how time is actually spent, and faces up to shortfalls in resources. It also ensures that quality standards are defined, and tries to evaluate the effectiveness and cost of various types of intervention. There is, in fact, something for everyone, service user, member of staff, manager and councillor. At the very least, it makes sure that decisions on which work is to be done and which can be left, are taken by councillors and managers, not by overstressed front line workers.

The analysis of the time and skills required to do certain tasks has another advantage — it can identify areas of activity which do not require the skills of the most experienced and qualified staff. These can be transferred to other staff without formal qualifications.

For example, one of Norfolk's early inspections was into the work being done by social workers approved under the Mental Health Act. We found that the vast majority of their time was being spent on problems relating to accommodation, welfare rights, employment and general advice on coping with day-to-day living. All these activities had been passed to the mental health worker because this was 'a mental health case'. We have no doubt that similar results would be found if a survey were done into the tasks of social workers dealing with children. Even accepting that a large part of childcare is dynamic enough to warrant an experienced and trained worker, there are still tasks and monitoring that can be carried out effectively by others under supervision. At a time when it is not uncommon for local authorities to have a vacancy rate for social workers of up to 15 per cent, it makes little sense not to analyse what only they can do, and to appoint others to make inroads into the rest. Vacancies and waiting lists do not deliver very good services!

To return to one of the inhibitions feared by some managers, namely that a workload management system would pass too much control to the staff. It can be seen from the above paragraphs that this would not be so. Decisions on standards and priorities will be left firmly with management and councillors. And of the quantity of work done? More work will be obtained from a workforce that is motivated to carry out achievable tasks than one demoralised through stress and overwork.

To complement a workload management system, management should also tell staff what they are to do if finance or other resources are not sufficient to deliver the service which has been assessed. Take the home-care service for example. Few Departments would be able to meet all requests for assistance within a cash-limited budget. To leave all decisions to the Home-Care Manager smacks more of abrogation of responsibility than delegation.

Or what of the Occupational Therapy Service? Again, a cash-limited budget with almost unending demands. Is the agency in the business of providing mugs, cutlery and bath mats which can easily be bought at the local store? That is not a decision for the occupational therapist, but the councillor.

A categorisation of needs in priority order by management and councillors, together with authorisation for the Home-Care Manager to deny a service to applicants in the lower need categories when money runs out, will ensure a standard which is understandable and achievable.

This issue will become even greater if authorities move into an assessor/provider split. If assessment is truly to be 'needs led', management must make it absolutely clear to the assessors what needs are going to be accepted as the responsibility of the agency to meet. For example, if an elderly man, living alone, cannot do his own shopping, but is visited each week by close relatives, who would be able to help him, but say that their community charge is so high thay they are going to get some return for it. The man needs his shopping done; but should the assessor accept that the agency will take that responsibiity from the family?

The heading of this section is 'Time, space and equipment'. So far, we have diverted a little from our discussion on making sure that staff have enough time to do a proper job into the area of utilising time to the best advantage to service-users and the agency itself. What need we say about space and equipment? Not a lot, we would think!

The point has already been made above that workers cannot deliver high-quality services unless they have the equipment and surroundings which enable them to use their time and skills efficiently. There is a price to pay for inadequate working conditions over and above staff having to waste their time and skills. Through this book we have stressed that a system of quality assurance cannot be successfully introduced unless the workers 'own' quality and are motivated to deliver it. How can this be achieved in bad working conditions? Poor surroundings and inadequate tools give one message to the workforce: 'Management does not care about me and what I do.'

Checklist of main points in Chapter Seven

1. No one employed in a social care agency works totally in isolation. The whole organisation cannot pull together towards a common purpose if various workers operate in closed boxes and could not care less if that affected their colleagues.
2. If local authorities spent as much time encouraging and assisting private home owners to have an efficient 'assembly line' as they do in carrying out sporadic inspections, the quality of care in the independent sector would benefit.
3. In order to 'own' their part of the service, staff need to know not only what they are to do, but also why they are doing it and how their part fits into the whole. Such preparation cannot be skimped.
4. Ensuring that each member of staff has the skills necessary to do their particular job is a necessity not a luxury.
5. The more skilled the workforce, the less time and effort has to be spent on checking what they are doing.
6. Staff development is one of the prime functions of line managers.
7. Even with the best instruction and training, quality work will not be produced by workers who do not have enough time to do a proper job or who have inadequate working conditions and equipment. If the efficiency of the Chief Officer is enhanced by good working conditions, why not that of the workers as well?
8. Whenever there is an acknowledged shortfall in personnel or resources, the 'width' of an agency's activities sometimes has to be reduced in order to ensure that minimum 'quality' standards can be met.
9. A workload management system will ensure that staff concentrate on the agency's priorities and are not given more work than they can cope with.
10. If assessment is truly to be 'needs based', then management must make it absolutely clear to the assessors what needs are going to be accepted as the responsibility of the agency to meet.
11. Poor surroundings and inadequate tools give one message to the workforce: 'Management does not care about me and what I do.'

8 Monitoring and inspection

In contradiction to those who consider inspection and inspection units to be the main harbingers of quality, we believe that you will already have created the basics to deliver a good-quality service if you have set user-oriented aims and values and standards, and if a properly prepared and motivated workforce is in place. All that inspection will do is to give a snapshot of what is happening, so that you can see if things are working to your satisfaction.

Please do not misunderstand us. Monitoring and inspection *are* important ingredients of a quality system, but, in themselves, they do *not* produce quality. Indeed, unless they can be viewed positively by all concerned, they can even have an adverse effect on the service. Many staff already have a good idea of whether or not they are providing a good service, and they also have a pretty fair idea of what may be preventing it from improving. To have an outsider pointing to deficiencies is only helpful if there is confidence that action can be taken to overcome whatever is contributing to the problem — and this means more than telling staff to pull up their socks!

Providing the climate is right in the agency, there should be no problem. If both management and staff have, as one of their main objectives, to provide something which the service user values, then both should welcome anything which could point to improvements. Even if inspections do not discover any flaws which need correcting, it is still reassuring to know that the best possible service is being offered. But, if the workforce is suspicious of management's motives and does not believe that the difficulties which *they* face are going to be addressed, an inspection which merely points out deficiencies can only lead to demoralisation and further cynicism.

Over and over again in this book we have emphasised the need to bring staff along with management. And that means the relevant trade unions and professional associations as well. Before the sole inspector was appointed in Norfolk over 10 years ago, and before the inspection unit was set up, negotiations were held with trade unions in order to clarify the 'ground rules'. This was particularly important as, with the best will in the world, it is difficult for senior managers to consult with over 5000 staff individually, and we thought it very important to listen to staff fears and suggestions. We eventualy agreed with the unions that the inspections would look at the performance of management as well as the workforce, reports would be made public within the Department, no one would be named in a report, and nothing found out during an inspection would lead initially to disciplinary action — although management retained the right to refer back to the original findings if, following direction or training, the worker persisted in malpractice.

But, above all, we convinced the staff and unions that the whole purpose of an inspection was to improve the service for users and to attempt to overcome difficulties which were hampering staff. Finding out deficiencies is of no positive value unless action is taken to rectify them.

Monitoring

Monitoring can be defined as the day-to-day routine checking of what is going on. It notes divergencies from standards that have been set. We suggest that there are five main types of monitoring:

Monitoring by the workers themselves

They should be the first to know if they cannot do what is expected of them. In addition, they are in the best position to check on the work or processes which are passed on to them by others. Again, this presupposes that they know clearly the standards to which they are to perform. Procedural checklists (easily available and understood) should be agreed by management, but some of the most useful procedures have been drawn up by the staff themselves or have at least been the subject of consultation with them. If standards are to be fully absorbed and 'owned' by the workforce, to involve them in the process of setting them up can mean that you are already more than halfway there!

But discovering that something is amiss has to be followed by action necessary to put matters right. So, unless the procedure spells out an alternative course of action, the worker should be provided with access to someone who can find a solution or who can authorise the lower standard of performance. Those line managers who are always too busy to be available when their staff require them (and who don't nominate substitutes) are the enemies of quality. Leaving staff with an unsolved problem is disabling.

Monitoring by the line manager

Again, action which is close to the service user — or at least far closer than waiting for a visit from an inspection unit. Several methods are possible.

- Observation, especially in residential and daycare establishments, where the worker can be seen in action.
- Through the reading of records, providing, of course, staff know what they are supposed to be recording! But day books, logbooks, case-files, reviews and even seeing copies of correspondence helps to ensure that, without taking away staff initiative, an experienced manager can monitor what is going on.
- Supervision, and here by supervision we do not mean the rehearsal with the worker of everything they have been doing with a particular service user. That should be clear from monitoring by observation or through the records, reviews and correspondence. Only points of concern not immediately dealt with need to have an action replay. Rather, we mean checking with the worker if there are hurdles within the agency (or in other departments and agencies) which are hindering performance; workload assessment; stress levels; training requirements and a staff development programme; setting targets (for both worker and manager) and checking whether the targets set last time have been met; seeking creative ideas about how the service could be improved. In other words, we see supervision as concentrating on the inputs necessary to achieve operational targets, as we described in Chapter 6. And, above all, supervision should be checking on morale and whether there are factors which are inhibiting a positive climate. By the end of the session, the worker should feel that his or her contribution as an individual has been valued.

Monitoring through the collection of statistical information

A most obvious form of this will be financial. We all have to keep within the financial limits set for our part of the service, and our failure to do so could adversely affect our own service users (if the money runs out partway through the year) and, just as importantly, other users in respect of whom a service may have to be denied because of our overspend. Indeed, much of the financial information collected could be criticised as being for 'negative' reasons (i.e. to stop fiddling), but a more positive view would be to say that financial control, which leads to full value for money, will ensure the maximum finances being made available for services required by users.

Operational statistics can also reveal unusual trends which may require investigating. For example, if you have a policy that no child should remain in a children's home for more than 6 months, and the monthly statistical return shows an increasing number staying for up to a year, you have the makings of an interesting inspection.

For many years Norfolk produced monthly information on such issues as case-loads, referrals, numbers of admissions and discharges from care, numbers of children in various settings and their length of stay, staff turnover, numbers of people receiving home-care and the average hours they were receiving. This information was broken down per area and was shared throughout the county, so that local managers — as well as senior management — could compare and ask questions.

It would be possible to extend the collection of information indefinitely. We would recommend, however, that you don't! Senior managers might like to play around with figures, but,in our experience, the accuracy of statistics relies a great deal on whether the person providing them sees their relevance or value, and sees the results from time to time.

We believe it to be far better to keep a core of data which is collected regularly, and anything else could be sought (in prospect, please, not retrospect!) as a one-off exercise. For example, if the agency had a standard that no daycare attender had to remain on transport for more than 45 minutes, it would be far better to check on this by asking occasionally for journey times rather than receiving reams of paper each week. In any event, that is the sort of monitoring best done by the driver and the line manager.

Random sampling

Instead of looking at everything, the person doing the monitoring would check a few operations selected at random, and from that would have a good idea whether standards were being met. Just like the post office, for example, who might have a standard that 90 per cent of first-class letters would arrive at there destination the following day. It would be absurd to monitor every letter, so they select a few going to various cities. There is no reason why the management of an agency should not do the same. A simple example would be checking on the speed by which referrals were being dealt with. Rather than looking at every referral, it would suffice to check a far fewer number chosen at random.

Monitoring via the service user

Perhaps the most common way of obtaining the reaction of users is by means of formal inspections or through the complaints procedure. But service industries also use another way. Customers are given a form asking them to comment on the quality of the service they have received. Is there any reason why this should not be done from time to time in social care agencies?

Inspection

Inspection is a more formal activity, being an exmination in detail as to whether the aims and values of the organisation are being met, as well as whether standards are being achieved. It looks not only at the end products or outcomes, but also at the means of arriving at them. If an inspection is done properly, the work of senior management (and sometimes councillors) is scrutinised just as closely as that of the front-line staff.

The Department of Health has published *Inspecting for Quality* — guidance on practice for inspection units. Although primarily focused on inspecting residential care, it was envisaged that in time *all* social care activities would come under the remit of such sections.

Inspecting for quality rightly places inspection as a quality control process which exists as part of a wider quality system. In paragraphs 4.6 to 4.12 it identifies seven principles of good inspection:

- The inspection process should be rooted in explicit values and measurable standards which should be publicly available.
- The activities and processes of inspection should be anti-discriminatory. Staffing within the unit should reflect the equality of opportunity, anti-discriminatory and anti-racist strategies of the Social Services Department.
- The processes and activities of inspection...should be publicly visible through a variety of means which may include reports, press articles, public meetings, etc.
- The inspection process should be impartial in relation to all agencies, e.g. general public, elected members, home owners, service providers, users and carers.
- The inspection process should be able to demonstrate a consistent method of operation (e.g. consistent across services and over time).
- The inspection process should be based on the gathering of objective evidence which can be independently validated to demonstrate that the process is reliable and unprejudiced.
- Inspection processes should be flexible, allowing both for planned activity and also for the need to respond effectively to unforeseen demands. The inspection process should help to give protection to the user by ensuring the availability of an inspection service on a regular basis, sometimes unannounced, and when emergencies arise.

To these, we would add the principles that we discoverd empirically from the early days of our inspections described in Chapter 2:

- negotiations with trade unions and professional associations, in order to counter suspicions and fears;
- the value in having operational staff seconded to the inspection team for each piece of work;
- the necessity to involve service users.

So, how in Norfolk were inspection projects chosen? All inspections were authorised by the Directorate (Director, Deputy and Assistant Directors). Suggestions could come from any source, line managers, politicians, the inspectors themselves. When deciding whether a project would be accepted, the Directorate looked at the following reasons:

- inexplicable inconsistencies in levels of service delivery across the County;
- evidence of consumer dissatisfaction (either individually or from other organisations);
- if current Departmental policy or procedures were thought to be inhibiting what was felt by individual practitioners to be good professional practice, and these cannot be addressed by existing management processes;
- trends in outcomes which were inconsistent with Departmental policy (e.g. a rise in the number of children in care), or which fall below agreed standards;
- key areas of Departmental functioning which have not been reviewed for some time (e.g. abuse conferences).

A topic having been provisionally selected, the Inspectorate was charged to draw up a detailed scheme and timetable, which would be submitted to the Directorate for final approval. A proposal would have the following elements in it:

- The establishment of an inspection team which would include staff seconded from the operational and support sections.
- Negotiations and involvement of those being inspected, while the brief is being developed, in order to ensure the credibility and ownership of the outcomes.
- Acknowledgment of existing work or research in the appropriate field from other than internal inspections or by other national research.
- A statement of the standards against which the inspection would take place. (If those standards were non-existent, then the first task of the inspection team for the project would be to draft them for approval by the Directorate.)
- The setting out of how the views of consumers are obtained, whether they be staff, carers or service users.
- A programme of feedback to the staff involved.

The inspection itself would lead to the formulation of conclusions and recommendations, which would cover the clarity of directions, operational outcomes, satisfaction of consumers, identification of staff development and training issues, the match between demand and resources, possible changes to agreed standards and the morale of the workforce. The final report to the Directorate would also include suggestions about the implementation of recommendations and the eventual evaluation of the worth of the particular inspection. The Directorate would then publish its response to the Inspection Report, so that staff knew what would (and what would not) be done about it. It would be unusual for the full report to be placed before councillors, but they would be advised of the conclusions either directly or as part of a composite report.

Let us give a few examples of the 40 plus inspections which have been carried out in Norfolk:

An audit

An audit of the work done by the County's (then) 12 area teams of fieldworkers was undertaken in 1985 and 1986. The reason for the inspection was that we, as senior managers, really had no idea of the quality of work being offered by the various areas, and in addition we were being told by most area managers that their work was suffering, when contrasted with other areas, because of an imbalance of resources.

Standards were agreed concerning what professionally would appear to be good practice, on the time limits for referrals to be dealt with, physical conditions in the offices, use of time, and administrative procedures to be followed. Also examined were workloads, type of work on caseloads, sickness and other absences.

The inspection team had a core membership of the Inspector of Social Work, Principal Research Officer, Principal Administrative Officer and a clerk/admin. officer. For each of the 12 inspections were added two other social work staff. (At that stage, we were not so heavily into testing the views of service users!)

Each team looked at all the referrals coming into the office for a month, scrutinised the case files of the last six children and adults admitted to care, took a sample of the case files of each social worker, and looked at how time and work were being organised.

The exercise took more than 12 months to complete and provided invaluable information not only for senior management prior to a restructuring, but also to the areas themselves, who were able to look at their own work practices and compare them with other areas. Of particular value was the highlighting of unclear standards and aims. The whole exercise firmed up our thoughts about the necessity of setting up a Quality Control and Staff Development Section, which we did in 1988.

We are delighted that this piece of work won the *Social Work Magazine* Award for management initiatives.

'Tell us what it's really like'

This was the title of an inspection (sponsored by an Enterprise Award from *Community Care* Magazine) into life in the County Council's homes for elderly people.

The concept was to recruit volunteers above retirement age to live as a resident in every one of the County's 46 homes. We hadalready done inspections of observation, where inspectors lived in the home for 3 days and nights, but these did not really give us much insight into what the residents thought and felt.

Of particular importance when setting up this project was the winning of acceptance from the staff — and the Councillors who would have to consider what action to take if major deficiencies were identified. Accordingly, a Steering Group was set up, which included the Chairman of the Social Services Committee, representatives of NALGO and NUPE, Age Concern (Norfolk), a reporter from *Community Care*, as well as the relevant managerial and administrative staff from the Social Services Department.

Age Concern (Norfolk) found and vetted the volunteers, who were briefed and supported by Social Services Staff. All volunteers were paid £50 for staying five nights as residents, during which time they kept a diary of what they saw and their feelings and impressions. And when these diaries were read at the debriefing sessions, some proved to be very moving indeed.

What of the outcomes? Overall, it was encouraging to learn of the commitment of staff and the general contentment of most of the residents. But problems *were* identified, amongst which were the sense of powerlessness felt by the volunteers and how rigid routines were created not by the staff but by some of the other residents. On the more practical side was the feeling of isolation because there was not immediate, private and inexpensive access to telephones (the volunteers would have preferred a telephone in their bedrooms to a television).

Three years on, some of the volunteers are still in touch with the homes where they stayed, giving insights to staff. Of all the inspections done, this gave us the most food for thought.

Inspection report into reception, intake and assessment

This was carried out in 1988 after a major Departmental restructuring into specialisms. The inspection was to check whether, with the new arrangements, applicants for help were receiving a speedy and appropriate response. (Perhaps at this stage we should mention that, in line with our philosophy of delegation and encouraging staff to 'own' the standards that had been set, each District had been allowed to choose for itself how best to organise reception, intake and assessment. It was known that rural and urban areas had chosen differing models.)

During this inspection, one in ten of people who had sought a service during one particular month were contacted to see if they would be prepared to be interviewed in their own homes by an independent person. Well over half agreed.

May we recommend such an inspection as a salutary experience to those who think of organising services for the convenience of 'professionalism' of staff! Although much of what we found was reassuring, some of the intricate allocation arrangements just left the users cold. Next time you look at your recepion/intake arrangements, ask yourselves what does the service user want? Or even better, ask the service users themselves. Two things will be of particular interest to them — the physical surroundings of the office and the speed with which their problem is dealt with.

Meals inspection

In 1989, a comprehensive study of the provision of meals in the County's homes for elderly people was carried out by an inspection team comprising six members of staff and seven people who either were, or had been, residents in one of the County's homes. (Obviously not all members of the team examined each home, but with 46 establishments a large team was required.)

The inspection looked at hygiene and working practices relating to meal preparation; the levels of nutrition and value for money of meals served to residents; the adequacy of the service in meeting special needs; and the view of the residents about the quality, quantity and range of food.

Not only did members of the inspection team visit each home to sample meals and seek the views of residents, but also 437 residents completed a questionnaire regarding the quality of food provided.

One of the main rewards of this particular piece of work was that, for the first time, standards could be drawn up based on the ascertained views of service users rather than those of managers and staff.

Boarding out arrangements for children who had been sexually abused

For this inspection we joined forces with the Social Services Inspectorate, primarily because the subject was new and standards were still evolving. Whenever it would cause no distress (and with the agreement of the parties), interviews took place with the children themselves and their parents. Foster parents and social workers were automatically included.

The results made us challenge some of our cherished views, and forced us to address the problem again of how, in large rural areas, it is possible to satisfy the often conflicting demands of geography and personal need.

Supervision orders

This was another example of an inspection being carried out by more than one agency, in this particular case by Probation and Social Services.

The aims of the project were to establish what impact supervision orders were having on young people; whether there were significant differences in the making and implementation of such orders within, and between, the agencies; whether the policy statements made by both agencies were being met; and whether practice procedures established by both agencies were being followed.

The inspection produced agreed factual information which was invaluable in the subsequent drawing up of joint working policies and practices.

The needs of disabled children and their carers

The first aim of this project was to identify whether the outcomes of intervention had been appropriate to the needs of the child. The second was to see if there were significant differences in decision-making and access to resources across the specialisms (disabled children were the responsibility of the disability section). Several parents of disabled children participated in the project.

The result was that new standards were set and agreed by a joint planning team comprising health, education, social services and organisations representing parents.

We hope that these few examples will show the range of subjects that can be covered. Certainly, we believe that Norfolk has not tried to keep away from the difficult option. But, again, may we stress four points:

- Staff and their representative must have confidence that what is being done is for the ultimate benefit of the service user, and that their own problems will be heeded.
- Services should be examined from the point of view of those receiving them, and the best way to do this is to involve service users from the start. Consult them *before* the project is set up, not as some kind of afterthought.
- Councillors must give their full backing and be prepared to face up to criticisms as well as receive plaudits. Norfolk has been fortunate in the composition of its Social Services Committee.
- Inspections not only point to deficiencies, they also praise and reinforce good practice. When deficiences are identified, the role of the inspection team is to recommend realistic and achievable proposals for improvement, and these could be directed at councillors and senior management as well as front line staff.

The role of inspection units

To begin with, let us describe the role of the Inspection Unit in Norfolk, which was set up in 1988 (without the benefit of advice from the Department of Health).

The prime role of the inspectors in Norfolk is to ensure a high quality of service delivery based on common minimum standards. This is to be achieved by:

- developing the department's professional policies;
- ensuring that the staff are aware of them through producing and maintaining procedures;
- leading a programme of inspections into both professional and managerial matters of concern;
- identifying and carrying out appropriate actions (including staff development);
- providing expertise, advice and consultancy to all Departmental staff.

This means that each inspector will spend approximately half of her/his time on the following tasks.

- Keeping under review the Department's functioning, changes in legislation, new Government guidance, and research findings and other initiatives in each specialist field. The inspector will then draw the implications of these to the attention of the Directorate. Each inspector will keep in touch with developments in other specialities in order to ensure that matters which have a wider significance are fully addressed.
- Planning changes in Departmental policy to solve identified problems, to meet new needs or requirements, and positively influence standards of practice. The inspector will work jointly with Departmental operational staff and those in other agencies to establish agreed policy and, where appropriate, will lead working groups.
- Providing advice and consultation to all staff.
- Reviewing, developing and producing the Departmental Procedures Manual for her/his own specialism, to ensure that actions on line with policy are clear to staff.
- Carrying out specific tasks at the behest of the Directorate, e.g. a Departmental response to major disasters.

The other half of the inspector's time will be spent on preparing and carrying out inspections.

This is not the model followed by many agencies, who believe that, for Inspection Units to be totally independent, they should be expected to make no significant contribution to the policy and practice of the agency apart from their inspections. Indeed, criticisms have been levelled at the Norfolk model on the grounds that inspectors have sometimes to inspect their own handiwork, i.e. whether procedures they have drafted are adequate. Our answer to that specific point is that the inspector is only one member of the inspection team, and if the other members wished to criticise the procedures they would do so.

More generally, we believe that it is valuable for the inspectors to have this wider role not only for them but for the Department. They are seen to have a base in the practical reality of delivering services, a most important feature — for if they once gain the reputation of being 'from the ivory tower', their credibility and worth would diminish. For the agency, there is the advantage of value for money by reducing duplication; if the inspectors with their specialist knowledge did not use it in the ways outlined above, other people would have to be employed to provide the same knowledge.

Besides their inspection duties, Norfolk's Inspection Unit have done such pieces of work as:

- drawing up a comprehensive set of specifications for the provision of services, in order to meet the requirements of the *National Health Service and Community Care Act* 1990 and the relevant government Guidelines. There are, for example, detailed specifications for residential homes (which have been discussed with representatives of the independent sector), luncheon clubs, field social work and occupational therapy services. We are delighted that other agencies have thought them worth buying at £300 per set!
- producing a complaints procedure. The need for one had been identified during the inspection on reception, intake and assessment (see above), and gained impetus from the requirements of the *Community Care Act.* Inspectors took a lead in consulting widely with service users about what should be in the procedure, its language and how it should be brought to the attention of all those who were receiving services.

In its publication *Inspecting for Quality* the Department of Health in Section 4 discusses whether inspection and service development can rest in the same unit or section. It concludes in para 4.24:

> Much depends on the meaning given to the terms 'development' and 'advice and support'. On the one hand, inspectors will as a matter of course provide feedback to homes, both formally and informally, on the outcomes of the inspections, and this will include suggestions and recommendations for improving services. This can clearly be considered an advisory and supportive role. On the other hand enabling those

improvements to take place is clearly a developmental role and is primarily the business of line management.

And in 4.25 'In practice these distinctions may not always be easy to make...' With this we heartily agree! We accept the statement that one of the objects of inspection is to inform development (para 4.26), but we believe that this means more than sending a report to the relevant line manager. Even though the prime responsibility for the development of the skill of individuals will rest with the line manager, the corporate responsibility of the inspector to improve the level of performance of the agency precludes their being able to shrug off a shared responsibility. In any event, the inspector may well be the person with the deepest knowledge of the speciality — and will certainly be the person who knows most about the problem they have identified. It seems a waste of expertise not to involve them in either planning for change or implementing a detailed training or staff development package.

As para 4.27 accepts, when private homes are inspected, many of them do not have a line management, so the inspector may have to take on that role.

Perhaps the reluctance to involve inspectors in 'hands-on' ways of improving services stems from the misguided fear that you should not be involved in supporting people when you might ultimately have to take legal action against them. If that were the case, we might as well say goodbye to the Probation Service, who are duty bound to bring their clients back to Court if they do not respond to the advice being offered. The fear seems to reflect the attitude of some Children's Departments in the 1950s and 1960s, who would try to help families through 'family casework', and if they failed, they passed the case over to the NSPCC to bring the children to Court in order to 'preserve our relationship with the client'! More modern social work practice has shown that it is quite possible for social workers to try to support families, and, in the event of the parents' failing to protect the child, to arrange for it to be removed from home, and even work with the parents to resume care of it later.

The first task of the inspector is to identify ways in which standards can be improved. Wielding a big stick should only be a last resort. In the field of childcare, no one, to our knowledge, has suggested that standards would be best improved by inspectors going round families threatening to remove the children!

Registration of private and voluntary residential homes

Although this topic should weigh no more in a consideration of quality assurance systems than any other activity of a social care agency, the driving force of the *Registered Homes Act* (1984) has tended, in some authorities, to confine thinking about quality to the registration function. Indeed, many authorities still seem to be struggling with the inspection of their own residential homes, never mind the more complicated issues surrounding care in the community.

Inspecting for Quality in para 4.28 says:

> The combining of registration and inspection of private and voluntary homes would seem to make good sense as both are regulatory processes under the Registered Homes Act. Where these are combined with advice and support, it is important that inspection unit staff recognise the potential conflicts in these roles and make it clear to service providers when they are operating under formal powers.

We believe that this advice is too conservative. Advice and support should be a prime function of the Inspection Unit, and we see little danger of professional staff being swayed against doing their statutory duty because they try to be helpful.

The aim of Norfolk's Arm's Length Inspection Unit is to improve the quality of life for people living in residential homes managed by the statutory and independent sector. The tasks of the homes officer are defined as being twofold:

> One is to monitor and regulate, the other is to enable and develop. These two roles are seen to be entirely complementary and it would be unwise to abandon one in favour of the other. Our experience suggests that the advisory enabling role achieves the better outcome, i.e. to improve the quality of life for residents. This approach widens the scope for inspectors to find realistic solutions to the problems they have identified. At the same time they are in a position to use statutory powers as a last resort. We acknowledge that it may not be easy to combine the two roles, although there are examples in the social services field when these two roles are used at the same time, e.g. when we carry out our statutory responsibility with regard to children in need of care and towards people with mental illness, but at the same time we use our enabling role to support and assist them and their families.
>
> Isn't that what the *Children Act* 1989 is all about?
>
> Norfolk came to this conclusion for the following reasons:
>
> - Experience over many years of a very large private sector showed that inspection or the 'big stick' approach was ineffective in rooting out bad practice, except in a few, very extreme cases. For what sanctions has the local authority really got if there is a difference of opinion between the proprietor and the inspector on standards? Embarking on the process leading to possible deregistration is cumbersome, time-consuming, expensive and unlikely to succeed unless there is strong evidence of malpractice.

This is particularly the case in respect of possible ill-treatment of residents. The chances of the inspector actually witnessing incidents which could be put to a tribunal are slim — even the stupidest proprietor would restrain themselves during a visit. And where would the other evidence needed by a Tribunal come from? Complainants rarely are willing to be witnesses, whether they be residents, relatives or other professionals. Indeed, the number of homes that have been successfully deregistered for poor standards is a miniscule proportion of the total number operating — and we do not believe that this is because the others are all functioning at a high level. It is more that some of them are operating at a level just not low enough to take action against, or where sufficient evidence cannot be collected. It may not be irrelevant that many of the successful deregistering have been on grounds such as criminal convictions and failure to keep proper records rather than on the standards of care offered.

- If enabling/advising had a better chance of effecting improvements in the quality of care, where would it come from? Homes that were part of large organisations (such as local authorities, some national voluntry bodies and a handful of private firms) could seek that sort of help from the line management of the agency. But what of the individual proprietor?

There would appear to be two options. Either groups of proprietors join together for mutual assistance and guidance, or they would turn for help to those who are finding deficiencies in their standards of care, i.e. the homes inspectors. The first option may seem very attractive, and some of the Associations for Home Owners have attempted to do this, sometimes with some success. But to our knowledge no orgnisation has yet been able to provide the impetus for all its members to achieve a uniform high standard of quality. Too often in an organisation will get sucked into fighting pretty sterile political battles, rather than keeping quality as the main objective. Perhaps they should not be criticised for this; any trade organisation tends to try to safeguard the livelihoods of its members as a top priority. In any event, it would appear that many proprietors either do not join such associations, and if they do, are reluctant to give to their trade competitors an opportunity to become too involved in their business.

- The main reason, however, for combining enabling with inspection was to try to encourage the introduction of quality assurance systems into individual homes. As we have said in other parts of this book, there is nothing in the system we describe which could not be applied to a single home, unit or section. Norfolk's inspectors are well versed in quality assurance. It seemed a nonsense for them not to use that knowledge positively.

In particular, quality depends on the vision of managers and the competence and motivation of staff. Norfolk's managers see it as part of their role to try to encourage this. And not only in single establishments. For 10 years they have been involved in seminars for prospective proprietors; they have encouraged (and helped) the setting up of training courses; they have encouraged proprietors to join in the County Council's search for quality to an extent that representatives of Norfolk Residential Care Homes Association and the Association for Residential Mental Health were part of the working party chaired by one of the authors which produced Guidance on the interpretation of BS 5750.

One final thought on the work of Registration and Inspection Units. When checking on the suitability of the regime in a home, we suggest you look closely at the system of quality assurance which the proprietor intends to apply — if indeed there is one! A good system and a commitment to quality will do far more to improve the lot of residents than any amount of external inspections with clipboard and tape-measure.

Checklist of main points in Chapter Eight

1. Before inspectors were appointed in Norfolk, negotiations were held with trade unions in order to clarify the 'ground rules'.
2. The whole purpose of an inspection is to improve the service for users and to attempt to overcome difficulties which are hampering staff. Finding out deficiencies is of no positive value, unless action is taken to rectify them.
3. Monitoring (i.e. the day-to-day checking of what is actually going on) should take five forms: by the workers themselves; by their line managers; through the collection of statistical information; via random sampling; and from the consumer.
4. When carrying out formal inspections, there are great advantages in co-opting operational staff onto the team. It is vital to involve service users.
5. Services should be examined from the point of view of those receiving them, and the best way of doing this is to involve service users from the start. Consult them *before* the project is set up, not as some kind of afterthought.
6. An inspection will report on clarity of directions to staff, whether operational outcomes are being achieved, staff development and training issues, the match between demand and resources, possible changes to standards, and the morale of the workforce.
7. In local authorities, councillors must give their full backing and be prepared to face up to criticisms as well as receive plaudits.
8. We believe that the involvement of inspectors in the formulation of policy and practice in an agency increases their credibility and leads to considerable financial savings. The 'independence' of the Unit can be safeguarded by the involvement of front-line staff and service users in the inspections.
9. The task of the Homes Officer in Norfolk is twofold: one is to monitor and regulate, the other is to enable and develop. Over the years it has become obvious that the 'big stick' approach is ineffective in rooting out bad practice, except in a few very extreme cases.
10. Staff inspecting residential homes should look closely at the system of quality assurance which the proprietor intends to apply. A good system will do far more to improve the lot of residents than any amount of external inspections with clipboard and tape-measure.

9 Consumer satisfaction

Let us return at long last to the analogy of the car manufacturer. There is no point producing a car to the highest specifications if no one wants to buy it. Or even if people don't know you have produced it! And you will lose future customers, if current ones are dissatisfied with the after-sales service.

These comments also hold good for the delivery of social care. If the service is seen to be irrelevant to the real needs of users, or if proper information is not circulated about them, or if any user dissatisfaction is not handled with care, your product will have failed the tests of quality we have set ourselves.

In order to ensure that they are producing goods or a service which the consumer wants and values, commerce and industry try to involve the consumer at all stages of the process. It is only sensible so to do. A few of the ways they do it are:

- doing market research into the type and range of products or services the customer might want. They will try to find out how customers would prefer these to be met;
- testing new products by asking the opinions of consumers, and making modifications in the light of the responses;
- at the point of service delivery, making sure that customers know exactly what they are getting. Standards will be clearly described. Remember, one of the definitions of a quality assurance system is making sure that the users of the service receive what they have been promised. Industry makes its promises through information on packages or on accompanying leaflets and guarantees;
- making sure that potential consumers know that a product or service exists, usually through advertising;
- in case the consumer is not satisfied, the producer will have set out a speedy and effective way of dealing with complaints, and, just as importantly, efforts will have been made to inform the consumer of these rights.

One of the difficulties facing large social care agencies is to decide who exactly are the service users. Obviously, there are 'clients' i.e. those who seek assistance because they are in need of care or guidance. But the list does not end with them. In the preceding chapter we discussed the service to be offered to proprietors of private residential care homes. And, what of carers, voluntary groups and the expectations of the general public? The situation is even more complicated when we realise that the customers of many managers, trainers and staff are the workers directly employed by the department.

Fortunately, the basic principles of how to obtain consumer satisfaction apply to all these groups of people.

First, three quotes. The first comes from a speech by Sir William Utting, the former Chief Inspector of the Social Services Inspectorate, when, in 1988, he addressed the Annual Seminar of The Social Care Association:

> The clients of services are people first. People have equal human rights, regardless of their situation or abilities, and should be enabled to exercise control over their own lives, as far as possible, by means of real choice. Following this is the principle that people are unique, and their individual needs should be addressed in a way which reflects this. Recognising their perception of need is vital to the provision of appropriate care and support. Services which provide a standard package through 'block treatment' of people with widely varying needs are no longer acceptable.

The second, we have already quoted more fully from this speech of David Mellor in Chapter 1:

> To define good quality is not always easy, but I urge you to begin by listening to your clients.

(In parenthesis, may we suggest that, although the two quotes above referred to prime service users, you would find it interesting to add the words 'and staff' whenever clients are mentioned!)

The third quote comes from a Study of Consumer Participation for the Personal Social Services Council in 1977 by Rose Deakin of the Institute of Community Studies, and follows her research into a Social Services Department:

> There were almost no examples of Consumer Participation at the level of strategic planning... [and on the one example where views were sought] there is no structure for feeding such material up through the system, expect by some personal initiative of the social worker.

We wonder whether, in the age of the *Citizen's Charter*, we are any better at involving users than we were in 1977?

There are problems in trying to give the service user exactly what they might choose. We identify three problems:

● What the user might want is not on offer. Even Department of Health guidelines are liberally sprinkled with the caveat 'within available resources'. For example, what if an elderly man says, 'I accept that it is right now for me to go into a home, but I would like to go into the same one as my friend. It is a nice home. I know it costs about £75 per week more than the one round the corner, but it is where I want to spend my last years. Unlike my friend, I'm afraid that I cannot afford it, so will you please meet the bill? No doubt different local authorities would come up with differing answers.

But in addition to the obvious problem of finance (including the bludgeon of charge capping), there are other constraints. The service requested might well be one that goes against the political will. If a Council, for example, decides that it will only subsidise placements in residential care for people who cannot be supported or protected in any other way, what happens if an elderly lady says, 'I am lonely and frightened of living on my own. I know that I can look after myself physically, but I would prefer the companionship of being with others in a residential care home. I have heard what you have told me about day-care, clubs and voluntary visitors, but my mind is made up. I want to go into a home.' Will the lady get her way?

● Sometimes the professional standards set will be at variance with the wishes of consumers. This may be easily recognised in respect of children's behaviour and the sanctions which may be applied to them. And it is not uncommon in considerations of child protection or mental health, when the law is at variance with what the user would wish to do.

But there are other ways in which the professional view might override consumer preferences. The agency, for example, might have set as a standard that no child would remain in residential care for longer than 6 months. What would happen if the parents refused to allow their child to be placed with a family other than themselves, and they had persuaded their young child not to co-operate with the plans? Would the child have to remain in a children's home, perhaps for the rest of his childhood, or would the professional view of what constituted 'best interests' prevail.

We are sure that you can think of many other examples where the task of the social worker is to discuss a range of options with the service user, but, in doing so, would exclude on professional grounds the choices which the user might prefer.

● The third inhibition is an extension of the 'professionalism' outlined above. More years ago than we care to remember, when the authors took their qualifications, much was made of the 'professionalism' of social work. The professions were said to have a body of knowledge, which was passed on to operators who in turn would use it to assess what people needed. The professional then tried to satisfy a person's needs rather than what they thought they wanted. A criminal might 'want' to be got off; the solicitor would try to provide a fair hearing of his case. The patient might want sleeping pills; the doctor knows that he or she needs counselling to adjust to a bereavement. It was left to tradesmen to give people what they wanted. They didn't assess what you really required; if you asked for it, you got it.

So far, so good. We accept that one of the skills of social work is being able to assess — with a person — what the needs are. Where social work can go wrong is if it also assumes the arrogance exhibited by the worst types of professionals and tries to impose solutions on people which might be theoretically correct but which are not endorsed by the user. We all know of medicine cupboards full of untaken prescriptions, but what of the unused walking frames, the uneaten meals, the attender at a day-centre who came because she did not want to upset her social worker, the resident who 'doesn't want to be any trouble' so he does what he thinks the staff want him to do?

It is right that social workers share their view of 'needs' with a service user, and then discuss all realistic ways of overcoming them. The skill of the social worker is not to manipulate 'the client' into accepting what the social worker thinks is the best solution, but in finding ways forward which can be 'owned' (yes, that word again!) by the user. That could mean accepting a solution which the professional personally thinks is second best, but which the user prefers. 'Professionalism' should not be allowed to inhibit user preference, unless such choices cannot be implemented for the reasons we have discussed above.

So much for the negatives! Let us now look at the ways that service users can be involved in a quality assurance system. Indeed, more than *can*; in many instances it is *should*, because of recent legislation and guidance which make it obligatory that users are consulted and informed.

Designing the service

Section 46 of the *National Health Service and Community Care Act* requires local authorities to publish 'community care plans' by April 1992. Before publishing them, the authorities are to consult with — amongst others — voluntary organisations representing service users and carers. These consultations are to:

- assist them in identifying the care needs of the local population;
- enable them to assess the services which are currently available;
- help to identify services which could be stimulated in response to their assessments of the care of the local population.

This corresponds to the manufacturer 'researching the market'. It makes a good deal of sense to ask the user to comment on the shape of future services before you plan to provide them.

But how is this consultation to take place? Some voluntary organisations these days find themselves in a quandary. Are they to campaign and fight on behalf of service uses and carers, perhaps making some independent direct provision which reflects the needs of their members? Or, if they are dependent on money from the local authority, will they have to enter into contracts with statutory agencies who will then hold the whip-hand over what they are to do? If they take the latter course and are tied financially to the local authority, how well will they be able to be independent advocates for their members.

Chris Heginbottom's book *Return to the Community* debates such problems and concludes that voluntary organisations will have to change their present way of thinking in order to create interlocking webs of community services which users actively participate in shaping and so fulfil the potential of their citizenship. They will then have to address the tensions of being both service provider and advocate, and establish positive relationships with the statutory sector based on clearer principles and objectives. In turn this vision of choice and consumerism will only work if local and central government are serious about guaranteeing assistance to voluntary organisations.

Chris Heginbottom is 'spot-on' with his analysis. Local authorities have to accept that if, as part of a quality assurance system, they wish to hear the independent view of the service user, they have to be serious about encouraging, enabling and even supporting agencies which are able to do it. The dilemmas facing some voluntary agencies is acute, and will only be resolved if local autorities are prepared to allocate funds without insisting on calling the tune all the time. When an industrialist pays for market surveys, he wants the truth as the consumer see it; he does not want the research company only to come up with sycophantic words of comfort.

Assuming that its attitude is right in its search for consultation, the local authority has several ways of engaging users in a debate on the design of the service. The first is quite simply to ask relevant groups for their opinions on present services and for their future hopes — but to do this before the dye is already cast. There is no point in consulting on strategy, if the decisions have already been taken. Be honest, and let people know what is up for debate and what is not. It is also important — especially for those organisations which do not have a paid secretariat — to give a timescale which allows voluntary members the opportunity to consult their members. It is no good sending out a paper on Monday which is due to be debated by a Council Committee on Friday! And when views have been given by an organisation, do have the courtesy not only to reply but also to explain the reasons why some of the advice might be accepted and why some might not.

We prefer direct contact with each relevant organisation, even if only by letter. There are large numbers of voluntary organisations because the needs of users and carers are different. It is false economy to think that one of them will adequately represent the rest. The token membership of a single organisation on a Social Services Committee or a Joint Planning Group may be helpful in obtaining one view, but do not deceive yourselves into thinking it will be more than that, unless that organisation has a formal system of passing information around all voluntary groups, of discussion comments, of reaching an agreed response and with the authority to represent that response.

All this is common sense, and will come right if the local authority does not see consultation as a hurdle to be overcome before it does what it wants to do, but more of a helpful way of designing a service. Exactly the same comments can be made in respect of consultation with staff and trade unions.

You will recall that, earlier, we commented that, among service users, can be proprietors of private residential homes. As an example of consultation, Norfolk sent out its draft of a revised *Guide to Registration* to each of the four associations which represented proprietors, believing — quite rightly — that no *one* would represent the views of the rest. The responses varied from 'Yes, we like it, but could you please consider...', through 'In general it's OK, but can we please discuss the following issues...', to annoyance for not having been consulted before the draft was drawn up and no reply. Those organisations which were prepared to discuss it were successful in effecting some changes, and the Guide was improved. The County Council also benefited because representatives of a large number of proprietors had helped us to circumnavigate some of the issues which would have caused difficulty amongst home owners and therefore caused preventable friction. The new Advisory Committees on Residential Care set up at the behest of the Department of Health to advise local authorities on how they should be carrying out their registration and inspection functions will provide a formal arena for consultation, but we would still advise direct contact with individual organisations — just as you would not consult with disabled people via voluntary groups only.

It is possible to involve individual service users in developing service designs? We believe it is, but only if they are accepted as giving an individual viewpoint or comment. There is no reason why working groups drafting a design for services should not have a service user (and a front-line worker) to give a practical perspective. But this is not a substitute for subsequent consultations.

Do the right people get consulted? Circulating documents to voluntary organisations is all well and good, but very many service users and their carers do not belong to any such group. And what of the general public, who also might wish to have a say? In an attempt to overcome this difficulty, Norfolk Social Services and the *Eastern Daily*

Press produced a four-page supplement of the draft Community Care Plan, which the newspaper inserted into all copies on one morning. Other items were broadcast on local radio, and, in both instances, people were told how they could make their views heard. Even if not many people did comment, many more would have a better idea of what the department was trying to do; and, as we will see later, informing people is part of the process of quality assurance.

A further way of involving users in the design of the service is by assessors of need making careful note of what services the user requires, but which for whatever reason cannot be delivered. That is easy! The more difficult bit is creating a channel through which that information can be collected by someone who has a brief to do something with it. A list of unmet need is of no use unless it is fed into the planning process.

Setting standards and inspecting them

Inspecting for Quality (Guidance produced by the Department of Health) says that standards in social care agencies should be developed via discussions with users and providers; local standards should increasingly emphasise the quality of life of service users.

Acknowledging that overall standards will ultimately be set by whoever assesses or purchases services, they would be unwise to try to do this without gaining the views of users about their appropriateness or the provider about their feasibility and cost-effectiveness.

This will be a cyclical process. In Norfolk, we have found that the best way of obtaining the views of users is during inspections; but before an inspection takes place, standards must be set against which services are to be measured. We therefore came to the conclusion that the standards for the earliest inspections would be culled primarily from existing policies and from guidance issued by the Department of Health and the Social Services Inspectorate, plus, of course, reports such as 'Home Life' and that produced on residential care by the committee chaired by Lady Wagner. Whether these were appropriate would be discovered during our inspections.

Seeking the views of users is a 'must' in all inspections involving service delivery. We accept that some inspections (e.g. into the quality of staff training or the climate of the organisation) can do without, but not where users receive a service. Indeed, we would go further and say that, wherever possible, users or their representatives should be included in the team of inspectors.

Throughout this book we have given examples of user involvement in inspections: elderly people being paid to live in our residential homes; people seeking help for the first time being interviewed in the inspection on intake, abused children, their parents and foster-parents being interviewed; 'tasters' being asked to comment on the quality of meals.

All these gave insights into services which were difficult for the 'professional' staff to have. And these insights were used to review the standards which had been cobbled together in the first place.

The use of service users and their advocates has also had another benefit. It has provided a source of information and comment which can be tapped before further changes to standards are considered. There is no longer any need to wait for an inspection to take place; we have people on whom we can test our ideas. And we have been able to draw some service users into training sessions for staff, so that the users' view can be given at first-hand.

Service delivery

The involvement of users in the tailoring of services is well put in two paragraphs of *Community Care in the Next Decade and Beyond* produced by the Department of Health in 1990.

> 3.16. The individual service user and normally, with his or her consent, any carers should be involved throughout the assessment and care management process. They should feel that the process is aimed at meeting their wishes. Where a user is unable to participate actively, it is even more important that he or she should be helped to understand what is involved and the intended outcome.
>
> 3.17. It may be possible for some service users to play an active part in their own care management, for example, assuming responsibility for the day-to-day management of their carers may help to meet the aspirations of severely disabled people to be as independent as possible.

Two major points emerge from these paragraphs:

- You may have the willingness to consult, but how do you ensure that the user is able to give their view if they have major difficulties in communication? This is one of the major points made in *Breaking Through*, a guide towards better service for deaf-blind people. Have the people who are to do the assessments the ability to communicate fully with the potential service user? The problem is compounded if the assessor always relies on the carer to interpret. What if the deaf-blind person has different opinions to the carer? It is a pity that the appointment of advocates for people with disabilities has had such a patchy acceptance. We may not like what the advocate is saying on behalf of the disabled person, but that may be the only way of learning what the service user really wants. A similar problem may be present when discussing the needs of a person with learning difficulties.

The solution to this problem is not easy. Norfolk has started to address it by increasing the number of guide-helps who can communicate with deaf-blind people, and to fund organisations, one of whose roles would be to be the mouthpiece of people with communication difficulties. But much more still needs to be done when resources permit.

- The bureaucractic processes involved in allowing a disabled person to have control over the money with which to buy help are enormous. One has to have a sympathetic and creative finance officer to make it work! Disabled Living allowances are often not enough, (even if this source proves adequate, the disabled person may well require a great deal of help in hiring staff and complying with good practices in personnel management and financial accounting).

But what if extra money is still required. Few local authorities seem keen to hand over sums of money to individuals. All sorts of deviations are practised, e.g. considering the disabled person an 'agency' and making payments from the agency budget, or allocating a number of homecare hours and allowing the user to choose and deploy their own staff, who nonetheless remain on the books of the Social Services Department. Perhaps the simplest method is to form (or even cause to be formed) a charity or voluntary organisation which can act as a middle man and to which the necessary finance can be given.

But despite administrative difficulties, the principle of involving the user to the maximum is a keystone of any system of quality assurance.

An interesting example of how services can be rethought following consultation comes from South Norfolk. The Social Services Department had, for many years, been allocated by the Education Department a (small but welcome) number of hours to use for Further Education. These had been used largely in established homes and day-centres. The Education Department was, however, worried that a relatively small number of disabled people were attending their mainstream evening classes.

Invitations to a meeting were sent to disabled people in the district to see if they agreed with the present provision. A reassuring number responded. The outcome was that many people with disabilities would have loved to attend some mainstream courses, but did not have the confidence to try. The meeting agreed that some of the 'social services' hours would be used to give preliminary booster sessions for disabled people, with a view to their being introduced into the mainstream as soon as possible. It has worked!

Informing the service user

Dare we refer to this as advertising?

Again, a quote from *Community Care in the Next Decade and Beyond.*

> 3.18. To enable users and carers to exercise genuine choice and participate in the assessment of their care needs and in the making of arrangements for meeting those needs, local authorities should publish readily accessible information about their care services.

This advice follows the strictures contained in the *Disabled Persons Act* (1986) and the *Children Act* 1989. Section 9 of the former states that a local authority has a duty to inform disabled people, on request, of relevant services, provided either by the local authorities themselves or by any other authorities or organisations.

The *Children Act* 1989 defines a new range of services for 'children in need', a definition which now encompasses children with disabilities. These services include day-care outside normal school time, help in the home, laundry services, respite care/holidays, family support and counselling. These services *must* be brought to the attention of carers and not just when a request for a specific service is received.

For the purposes of quality assurance, we do not think there is any further value in our labouring this point. It should be self-evident that, unless users know what is on offer, they cannot be expected to make informed choices; and, without informed choices, they are unlikely to 'own' the service which is eventually provided. Without that ownership, the chances of user satisfaction are that much slimmer.

Some agencies might feel reluctance at advertising services which are under pressure already. We would argue that, if your prime objective is to satisfy those in the greatest need, you cannot be sure you are doing this, unless you are confident that such people know of the existence of services. Rationing through ignorance seems to be a recipe for political as well as personal distress. If resources prove not to be sufficient, other action is always possible, such as reviewing standards and withdrawing services from those in the least need — but more of that in a subsequent chapter!

After care services

Just as manufacturers continue to look after their customers after a sale, so in any system of quality assurance does the social care agency. In particular, the user should know what to do if the agreed service does not come up to expectations.

How to deal with complaints is spelled out in both the *National Health and Community Care Act* and in the *Children Act* 1989. The setting up of complaints procedures is compulsory, and the involvement of an independent element is a necessity. For your interest, we enclose in the Appendices a copy of a leaflet setting out Norfolk's procedure — although we suspect that this differs little from those of other authorities.

How far the complaints procedure is to be 'pushed' is a matter of local determination. Whereas it is absolutely right that dissatisfied users know of their rights, there is also a danger that, used prematurely, the complaints procedure can undermine the confidence and morale of the workforce. We have heard of some agencies where the first action of a visiting assessor is to hand over a leaflet outlining the complaints procedure!

Can you imagine your own reaction if you went into a shop to buy a television, and before helping you to choose a set, the salesman pointed out what would happen if the set went wrong or how you could complain if you didn't like his attitude? We bet that most of you would make your excuses and leave! It hardly encourages a positive and confident response if the first thing talked about is failure! Far better, in our opinion, for the subject to be raised when a package of care has been agreed, or if agreement appears unlikely.

How senior managers and councillors respond to complaints is a very delicate issue. The first priority must be to ascertain whether the user has or has not been dealt with fairly in accordance with the standards that have been set. But they should also have in the forefront of their minds the climate of the organisation — you remember, the morale of staff, their enthusiasm, their pride in their job. Little is more demoralising to the workforce than a feeling that complainants are always believed, and that staff are guilty until proved innocent. Management would do well to remember that they may be dealing with some of the most disturbed, disgruntled and even deviant people in their locality — and we are not referring to their staff!

Managers and councillors should also be wary about changing standards just for one complainant. According to government guidelines, users and carers can complain about the services which are not on offer as well as those that are in operation. In other words they can complain, for example, that the local authority has a policy of only supporting financial placements in independent residential homes in cases where a user requires protection. A parent (and the child) might wish their adult child to have more independence from the family, and therefore is seeking a placement in an independent residential home. This is not life and limb, and the assessing officer rightly might have turned down the application in the light of the standards they had been set. It would be appalling for staff morale, if, in order to obviate possible bad publicity, senior managers allowed the appeal but did nothing about the original standard.

Similarly, to allow an appeal merely because it is supported by an MP or a councillor will ultimately do a great deal of harm to the overall quality of a service. As we have said before, cynicism amongst staff is one of the worst enemies of quality.

In social care, the customer is not always right!

Empowerment

To some extent, what we have been describing above are the elements of what is described in other places as 'empowerment'. In other words, part of the system for quality assurance is giving to the service user more opportunities to influence, and even control, what is happening.

No longer is the service provider (and the assessor of services) saying that he or she knows best and is the only person with the ability to control what is going on. Just as the potential buyer of a car is credited with the ability to choose the model that is most suitable, so is the user of social care. The task of the assessor is to enable the potential user to exercise choice by providing the best knowledge and information about the various options that are available, and even more importantly to see whether, between them, the assessor and user can work out a better alternative to anything presently on offer.

But to do this, the assessor has to be given the authority to use imagination. (Remember the climate of the agency!)

This is particularly relevant when help is to be offered to someone whose pattern of life may be considerably different from those who provide the services. Does it not make sense to allow the user, or the carer, or groups of people of similar interest and lifestyle to choose, or even organise, the care that is most appropriate?

Within the constraints already alluded to earlier in this chapter, 'empowerment' is a concept which lies at the heart of any quality assurance system.

Perhaps at some time 'empowerment' will have its day. Vested interests may be overcome. It is not easy for those in power to relinquish any of their control, and specious arguments about democratic accountability are used to bolster the status quo.

But the measures suggested in this chapter will bring that day nearer. Involving users in the planning, not only of their own care but for more general services, will tailor services more in keeping with actual needs. Realistic consultation and feedback about services on offer will lead to improvements. Inviting users on to inspections will again make the results more sensitive.

By harnessing the power of users in this way, the chances of user satisfaction will be increased. And that is what quality assurance is all about.

Checklist of main points in Chapter Nine

1. Your services will have failed the test of quality if:

   - they are seen to be irrelevant to the real needs of users;
   - proper information is not circulated about them;
   - user dissatisfaction is not handled with care.

2. Service users should be involved at all stages of the quality assurance process.
3. Legislation and Government guidance require consultation with service users and carers in the following areas:

   - planning services (The Community Care Plan);
   - setting standards and inspecting them;
   - assessment of need and care management.

4. In addition, service users now have a right to know what services are on offer, and how to complain if they are dissatisfied.
5. Involvement of service users does not mean that they will necessarily get what they want. It does, however, mean that their views are always taken into account and that they are fully informed about what is happening.
6. Just as staff need to 'own' what they are doing and have some control over their activities, so the service user should be similarly empowered.
7. This empowerment not only will lead to greater user satisfaction, but will overcome some of the discriminations met by minority groups.

10 Review of the system

The attempt to improve the service we are giving should never stop. Needs change, knowledge and resources fluctuate, new legislation forces fresh responses, and, most of all, the expectations of service users and the man or woman in the street are not static. A major part of a system for quality assurance is a regular review to ensure that all its parts are functioning and relevant.

In this chapter we shall look at the stages in the system we have already described and point out where reviews are imperative. It should go without saying that the object of the review is not just to evaluate what is going on; there should also be the commitment to do something about any deficiencies found.

Review of the departmental climate

In our experience, this is one of the most neglected, yet most vital, areas for almost continuous scrutiny. We cannot stress enough that no system for quality can be developed effectively unless an organisation cultivates the attitudes of enthusiasm, imagination, maximisation, consultation and pride in the job and in the organisation. Indeed, the developing of such a culture should be addressed before a system of quality assurance is introduced.

The factors that can be considered are spelled out in Chapter 4. But how is one to review a 'climate'?

Information can be obtained in the following ways:

Through line managers

They are in the forefront of all the organisation's operations, and should be in a good position to assess the morale of the workforce and identify what, in the policies and procedures, might be hampering the development of a proper climate. Even accepting that the main way of receiving views from them should be through the management 'chain of command', regular meetings between the directorate and line managers would give an extra dimension to the usual channels.

During inspections

The motivation of staff and their ability to use their initiative should always be on the agenda of the inspection team. And, even if staff may be reluctant to disclose their feelings to line managers and full-time inspectors, there is at least a chance that they will do so to a fellow worker, if — as we have recommended — such a person is a member of the team.

Via trade unions and professional associations

Yes, we know that they may have their own agenda. But if they have been brought into discussions about a quality assurance system at an early stage, and can see the advantages to their members of a system that works, they can be a useful extra channel of communication between management and staff. (Note that we said *extra.* Meetings with trade unions should in no way detract from the importance of managers communicating directly with their workforce.)

Senior officers finding out for themselves 'what it is really like'

We are not suggesting that, if a Director of Social Services spends a day in an area team or residential establishment, staff will unburden their innermost feelings! No, but if she/ he from time to time looked at pieces of work from the viewpoint of front-line worker, and followed the administrative processes that have been laid down, fresh insights might follow about whether staff are being allowed to use initiative and whether the procedures are more of a hindrance than a help. So, yes, for senior staff to spend a few days on intake/reception might work wonders!

From external consultants

One of the authors has been a member of four teams from the Health Advisory Service, which visit health authorities and social services departments to advise on provision of services for people with mental health problems and for elderly people. During the visits, staff of all grades are seen, many of whom are delighted at the opportunity to give their views to outsiders. We believe that a few hundred pounds spent on asking an outsider to review the climate of the organisation would be money well spent.

Review of aims and values

Here we refer not only to the aims and values of the whole agency, but also of specific units, sections and establishments.

It may be thought wrongly that the aims and values are immutable. Far from it! External policy shifts by government, developing professionalism, media attention and the changing expectations of users and carers all can lead to changes in what agencies do and why they are doing it. Let us look at a few at random:

- The emphasis in user involvement and in ensuring quality would not have found much space in Mission Statements of 10 years ago.
- The balance between parental responsibilities and the protection of children changed after the Butler-Schloss Inquiry.
- The role of the local authority as being sole provider changed to being the enabler and promoter of some services.
- The restrictions in finances has resulted in some agencies redefining what they are in the business of doing.
- In respect of childrem with severe learning difficulties, accommodation is sought in foster homes and community homes rather than in hospitals.
- Issues concerning equality are higher on the agenda, and positive discrimination is acceptable.
- The possibility of users directing their own care programmes is being explored.
- During the last 20 years, society has changed its attitudes to adults with learning difficulties. Who, at that time, would have offered advice on sexuality?
- The concept of 'shared care' has been promoted by the *Children Act* 1989.
- Elderly people with greater degrees of frailty and confusion are now being accommodated in homes for elderly people rather than being admitted to hospitals.

We suggest an annual review of your statements of aims and values. There may be more changes than you might imagine.

Review of standards

Whether standards are being reached should be checked constantly through the process of monitoring.

Inspections, by definition, are more detailed reviews of whether standards are being achieved, and whether, in fact, they are achievable. If there are problems, the inspection would recommend what action needs to be taken — usually either to help staff or to change the standard required.

When an inspection is first set up, those inspecting have to be clear about the standards they are to evaluate. If standards are lacking, do not exist, or are poorly defined, the inspection team has to agree some with the operational managers and staff. So, a review of standards takes place before each inspection.

If the inspectors find that standards are not being met, they can either identify the cause and make recommendations to put it right (e.g. organisation of work, clarity of instruction, staff training) or they can conclude that the standard is unattainable within the resourcing and skill levels available. That is when senior managers and politicians have to review the standards. The stark choice is often to find the money or change the standard. Few agencies seem prepared to do this kind of review on a systematic basis. It is far more comforting to try to muddle through, but, in the end, front-line staff will be left taking the unpopular decisions unless those in charge are prepared to take a lead. And, once that happens, the scene is set for conflict.

Review of monitoring and inspection

One of the main objectives in any system of quality assurance is to ensure that action is taken to correct whatever mistakes or faults are found. In addition to putting things right for the individual service user, it is also necessary to make sure that the mistake is not repeated for others.

The complaints procedure may highlight deficiencies. If that happens, it makes sense to hold a review of the present monitoring arrangements to ascertain why the problem was not picked up at a stage earlier than following a complaint by a user. Is there an adequate 'checklist' of action? Did the worker, in fact, identify difficulties which management failed to resolve?

Perhaps the problem involved a lack of resources. Did management and the councillors know of this? Is the management information system sophisticated enough to show unmet need in a way which can be used?

If inspections show failures in operation, monitoring processes should be examined as part of the work of the inspection team.

From time to time, there will be matters of grave public concern — perhaps following the untoward death of someone who was receiving a service. A full-scale review will be held not only of the monitoring processes but also the whole system of quality assurance which is designed to minimise such occurrences. Again, just as with complaints, this has to be handled with great sensitivity by management. Despite everyone's best endeavours, tragedies will occur, and staff involved could feel angry, depressed, guilty — a whole range of emotions. The morale not only of the workers involved but also of the whole agency might depend on the attitude taken by management to the incident. Is the first reaction supportive, with the offer of counselling and help? Or is it to plunge in to see if there are any grounds for disciplinary action being taken against a colleague? It may be a truism to say that an agency which cannot care for its staff, when they are in difficulty, should not be in the business of offering care to others.

And, finally, there needs to be a periodic review of the work and worth of the inspection unit. No doubt, the leader of such a unit could come up constantly with a good case for the expansion of her/his empire. There are always areas that could, with benefit, be inspected, are there not? And standards that require review and modification? Inspection units can be expensive, especially if agencies do not augment the core inspectors with operational staff. Is the agency getting full value for money? Have inspection reports led to improvements in service? In our view, a balance has to be struck between the money spent in finding out that problems exist, and putting solutions into effect. Remember, it is the workforce that produces a quality service, not inspectors.

Review of the whole system of quality assurance

To quote from the Roman poet, Juvenal: 'Quis custodiet ipsos custodes? — who will guard the guards?'. Who, indeed, will inspect the inspectors?

Periodically, your whole system should have an external MOT. Perhaps the Social Services Inspectorate would see this as one of their roles. Or reciprocal arrangements could be reached with another agency to inspect each other. As a last resort, you might even call in external consultants!

An exciting new idea of how to review the whole system is, however, being developed by The Social Care Agencies Quality Sector Committee of the British Quality Association in conjuction with Norfolk County Council. To satisfy the training need for registered assessor auditors, these two agencies jointly put together a 5-day training course which was run in association with Stebbings and Partners International.

This course aimed to provide a basic working knowledge of the skills involved in assessing quality systems and concluded with an examination recognised by the Institute of Quality Assurance as meeting the training requirement for registration as a lead assessor. This is a step towards creating a nationwide quality auditing network.

But before you can review your system, you have to set one up in the first place!

Checklist of main points in Chapter Ten

1. A major part of a system for quality assurance is a regular review to ensure that all its parts are functioning and relevant.
2. Of particular importance is a review of the climate of the organisation, as dispirited staff will not deliver a quality product no matter how good the system. There may be advantages of staff morale being checked by someone from outside the agency.
3. Needs change, knowledge and resources fluctuate, new legislation forces fresh responses, and, most of all, the expectations of the man or woman in the street are not static. Services are therefore never static. Aims, values and standards need to be examined regularly.
4. Check whether you are getting value for money from your inspection unit.
5. But before you can check on the effectiveness of your quality assurance system, you have first of all to set one up!

11 Postscript

Some of our readers may be surprised at the absence of much comment in this book about the concepts of purchaser/provider splits or case management.

This has been quite deliberate, as, in our view, such structural considerations are largely irrelevant to a discussion on quality assurance.

There are many ways in which social care agencies can organise themselves and still provide a quality service. A purchaser/provider split is one of them. But, in itself, it will not deliver quality. Indeed, unless it is coupled with a properly designed quality assurance system and is introduced into an agency with the right 'climate', it will probably fail.

It is sad that, in so many agencies, when managements diagnose problems in service delivery, they tend to tackle the symptoms rather than the cause. In other words, they will play around with structures instead of searching out why the workforce is not delivering the services required by both agency and user.

To recap on the main ingredients of a quality assurance system:

- A system for quality is driven by the needs of the service user.
- Everyone (i.e. councillor, user, manager, worker, man or woman in the street) should know what you mean by quality.
- The 'climate' of the organisation has to be prepared, and the essentials of enthusiam, imagination, maximisation, consultation and pride put into place.
- The workforce has to be properly motivated. It has to understand the system and own it as their own. Staff, unions and management need to build up trust in each other's desire to make it work.
- A clear statement of aims and values should be produced and widely published.
- Standards for service should be set at levels which are achievable by the workforce.
- All members of staff should have the resources, training, time, equipment and conditions to do the job expected of them.
- Monitoring should be done by the workers themselves, their line managers and, in an overall systematic way, by senior managers.

- Inspection should be seen by staff to be credible and knowledgeable about local conditions and difficulties. One way to do this is to incorporate front-line workers and users in the team. Inspectors should look at the performance of managers.
- The service should be advertised and should provide a system for rectifying justifiable complaints.
- Users, carers and their representatives should be heard at all stages of the system.
- All parts of the system should be subject of regular review, as indeed should the effectiveness of the system as a whole.

Whatever organisation you decide to adopt, the above need to be built into it, otherwise you are likely to be wasting your time.

The 'bottom-line' is for the service provider to offer what the user agrees meets his/her needs. Whether this is best done by creating a purchaser/provider split is a debate which we will not pursue here.

But, if an agency is thinking of following that course, there are several factors which they will have to overcome:

- Do the staff really understand what is entailed, and do they 'own' the change? Have you given enough time for the idea to be debated and absorbed by the people who will have to implement it? You know what the consequences will be if you haven't.
- Are you certain that the providers and purchasers both 'own' the same standards? A good purchaser will insist that the provider has a viable system for quality assurance. Both will be in constant contact with the user. Have you adequate mechanisms in place for changing specifications in the light of changing user requirements?
- What values are underpinning the service? Are finance and 'the contract' the all-important driving forces, or are user needs and professional interpretation?
- How do you intend to overcome the in-built duplication of assessment in the system? For, make no mistake about it, the provider will not 'own' the problem of the user, unless he/she is satisfied that the assessment has been done correctly.
- Are you sure that the problems of your organisation are such that the upheaval and extra administration provoked by the split warrant the time and effort involved.

May we make it clear that we have no axe to grind for, or against, the creation of a purchaser/provider split. We are, however, worried about the speed with which many agencies are espousing it without properly understanding all the implications.

One final thought on this issue. In our discussions with representatives of some agencies, we have noticed a disconcerting intent to 'distance' the purchasers of a service from the providers. This is apparently to preserve the financial integrity of the system for allocating contracts.

In our view — and indeed in the view of the Department of Trade and Industry — this will run counter to the best way of achieving quality. May we once again quote Clive Bone:

> In the industrial world the setting of standards can be a joint exercise as between purchaser and supplier. This does not usually lead to poor quality. Far from it. It ensures that both know what is required...The advice given by the Government to the industrial sector advocates involving suppliers, for example, with product design. In respect of quality assurance the best relationship as between suppliers and purchasers in the view of the Government is very clear:
>
> - Tell all your suppliers clearly what your quality requirements are.
> - Help and train your suppliers to meet your quality requirements.
>
> The above is taken from *Managing into the 90's*, which is a Department of Trade document aimed at British industry.... The Government wants industry to adopt best international practice in order to survive, and best international practice demands a proactive client/purchaser role in the interests of service delivery. Or, to put it another way: 'Arms length' should not mean semi-detatched.

To quote Peter Sellers: 'And finally, in conclusion, our last words will be... .'

We cannot think of any successful major enterprise which does not have in place a system for quality assurance. The effort to introduce one should not be underestimated, for it involves every aspect of an agency's activities. A similarly concentrated effort is required to maintain and review the system, once it has been put in place. There is no quick fix.

All parties involved may have to give up some of their entrenched attitudes towards each other, and that will take time and courage. But, it can be done, provided each party can trust the others to have at the forefront of their aims an improving service for the user. And, depending on history, that trust may have to be earned.

The rewards will be great for everyone:

- Councillors and owners will know that what they have decided will actually be delivered efficiently and economically.
- Management will have a system which will accentuate positive work and gradually eliminate the poor and the negative.
- The workforce will have the time, space, training and equipment to do a proper job.
- Service users will receive the service which they have agreed is the best available to meet their needs.

We wonder why we did not think of it before we did?

Appendix 1: Mission statement – Wiltshire County Council

Introduction

The County Council exists in order to serve the people of Wiltshire. It must know what their needs are, and it must be organised to meet those needs in the most effective way.

Chief Officers have therefore prepared this Mission Statement setting out their approach to the tasks ahead. It will only have meaning if it is known to, and shared by, all who are involved in the work of the County Council so that its philosophy and values are reflected in their relationships not only with the public but with each other.

The Statement is being circulated to staff of the County Council. Your Chief Officer is arranging presentations to discuss it with staff. It is not the last word on the subject. Please think about the Statement carefully, and make your views known during your department's discussion process. All comments from departments will be considered by Chief Officers in July 1991.

The Statement

Our business is to…

- listen
- respond
- serve
- excel

to make Wiltshire *the* County in which to live and work.

In support of our Mission Statement we are committed to the following values.

Customers

We value our customers, the people of Wiltshire, and will deliver the services which meet their needs;

We must therefore:

- identify ways of ascertaining customer needs;
- develop with our staff best practices of customer care;
- monitor responsiveness of the organisation and standards of customer satisfaction.

Staff

We recognise that our staff are our most valuable asset and will enlist their total commitment through encouragement, involvement, training and job satisfaction.

We must therefore:

- make time to talk to staff and listen to their views;
- develop and implement the personal appraisal scheme;
- ensure that appropriate staff development and training opportunities are used;
- acknowledge the justifiable aspirations of staff for recognition and appropriate conditions of work, and strive to meet them.

Communications

We will listen and respond to our customers and staff. We will communicate with them clearly and openly so that the fullest understanding is achieved.

We must therefore:

- produce effective channels for two-way communications throughout the County Council, and with all members of staff;
- improve customer contact through shorter response times, acknowledgements, letter and telephone style, and proactive public relations;
- develop the use of information technology to provide the best management information and improve business efficiency;
- establish a county-wide information system which allows our customers easy access to all types of information about the County Council and its services, and allows comment on services without undue effort.

Quality

We will deliver our services promptly to the best possible quality and with value for money. We will seek constantly to improve service effectiveness.

We must therefore:

- introduce training courses about quality;
- specify clear standards and define conformity;
- make full use of opportunities afforded by independent monitoring, inspection and evaluation.

Innovation

We will encourage and welcome new ideas, acting upon those which will improve the effectiveness of services.

We must therefore:

- demonstrate to staff that new ideas are welcome and will be rewarded; act on suggestions that are practical and explain why others are rejected;
- create a climate in which innovation can flourish;
- implement a team approach to the generation of new ideas.

Leadership

We value energetic, committed and inspiring leadership which requires delegation with accountability, and encourages personal and professional development of all staff.

We must therefore:

- make sure that all staff know what they have to do, and what is expected of them;
- live up to the Mission Statement, associated values and action plans;
- examine our own performance and 'management style'.

Teamwork

We value the diverse and unique contribution of committed teamwork.
We must therefore:

- review the working of management teams and of other working groups;
- encourage staff to work together rather than in compartments;
- commit effort and resources to team-building.

Integrity

We value integrity in all our work, believing that the highest standards of personal and professional conduct are essential within the public service.
We must therefore:

- ensure that standards are in accord with the values and that there is an understanding by everyone that staff serve the County Council as a whole;
- by example, reinforce the highest standards of integrity and professional conduct throughout the service.

Enthusiasm

We value enthusiasm and effort believing that the encouragement of these qualities will enable our staff to enjoy their work and give of their best.

- We must therefore develop a sense of pride in the County Council and be enthusiastic about our work.

Appendix 2: If you need to complain... We need to listen — Norfolk Social Services

We want to hear what you have to say

We provide services in a variety of ways to try to help people. Our job is to deal with sensitive and delicate matters.

There will be occasions when things go wrong. It may be something simple that can easily be put right. But whatever the cause, when things go wrong it can be upsetting for everyone involved.

One of the ways we can protect your best interests is by having procedures which are followed by everyone who works for us.

These procedures outline the way our experience and our users tell us it is best to deal with different situations.

If these procedures are followed everyone knows exactly what ought to happen and what to expect.

If you need to complain, we need to listen. And to make sure that we hear, we have agreed procedures that will be followed whenever a complaint is made.

You have a right to complain

If you receive, or are entitled to receive, a service then you have a right to complain about the quality or nature of the services that we have offered or provided.

We don't like getting complaints any more than anyone else. But we do like to know when problems crop up so that they can be put right as soon as possible.

If you want to complain there are three basic steps in the process. These are outlined over the page. Our internal procedures on confidentiality mean that what you say will only be passed on to someone who needs to be involved in sorting the matter out.

You don't have to go through the whole process. Whenever you are satisfied that the matter has been cleared up, you can say so and the process will stop. Even so, it may be that some matters have been brought to our attention that we need to follow up ourselves.

Although most problems can be sorted out by talking them through, this is not always the case.

Our procedure is designed to make sure that all complaints are dealt with fairly and thoroughly.

If you would like someone to help you at any stage, we can put you in touch with independent people who will speak on your behalf, help with translation, or in any other way you want.

Who to contact

An Assistant Director oversees our Complaints Procedure. He is referred to throughout this leaflet as the Designated Officer. If you have any queries about how the procedure works, or if you have already made a written complaint and would like to know what stage it has reached you should contact him.

He is:

Mr Himu Gupta
Assistant Director (Quality Control)
Social Services Department
Norfolk County Council
County Hall
Martineau Lane
Norwich
NR1 2DH
Telephone: Norwich (0603) 223437.

Where you can reach us

Main office

Social Services Department
County Hall
Martineau Lane
Norwich NR1 2DH
Tel: Norwich 222141

District Offices

WEST NORFOLK
Regis House
Austin Street
King's Lynn
PE30 1TJ
Tel: King's Lynn 762731

NORTH NORFOLK
Northfield Road
North Walsham
NR28 0AS
Tel: N Walsham 500550

Council Offices
1 Baron's Close
Fakenham NR21 8BH
Tel: Fakenham 863241

BROADLAND
156 Thorpe Road
Norwich
NR1 1TJ
Tel: Norwich 660316

GREAT YARMOUTH
St. Nicholas Road
Great Yarmouth
NR31 0PH
Tel: Gt. Yarmouth 664282

BRECKLAND
31 Norwich Street
Dereham
NR19 1DH
Tel: Dereham 694711

NORWICH
Reception Team
Charing Cross Centre
St. John Maddermarket
Norwich
NR2 1DN
Tel: Norwich 223500

SOUTH NORFOLK
Aspland Road
Norwich
NR1 1SJ
Tel: Norwich 660456

Step One: an informal complaint

You can tell any of our staff about the problem. Obviously it is best if you can tell someone who knows and understands your situation. This may be the worker responsible for your case or it may be someone you deal with on a more regular basis. It can be anyone you want.

Whoever you choose, please make sure that you know their name and position in the Department. You may need to refer to them again.

They will listen very carefully to what you have to say. They will explain our complaints procedure, and answer any questions you may have about it.

It may be possible for things to be sorted out straight away. If so , so much the better.

But any member of our staff who receives a complaint will always tell their own supervisor about it.

The worker who is responsible for your case will also be told, and they will want to make sure that everything has been properly sorted out, and that you are satisfied with the outcome.

They will also make sure our Designated Officer knows about your comments. In this way we can pick out any trends there may be across our services or areas, and possibly improve the way we do things so that other people don't have similar difficulties.

But of course you may not be satisfied with the outcome…

Step Two: A formal complaint

If after hearing about the outcome of an informal complaint you are still unhappy with the situation, you have the right to make a formal complaint, in writing.

This should be addressed to the Designated Officer who will make sure that your complaint is investigated fairly and thoroughly. (His address is on the other side of this leaflet.)

Your letter need only give a brief outline of the problem and the name of the person you have already spoken to.

The Designated Officer will first of all check to make sure that all stages in Step One have been gone through.

If so, within a week of receiving your letter, the Designated Officer will let you know which senior member of the management team has been asked to take a closer look at your complaint. It will be either a District Manager or an Assistant Director who has not previously been involved with your case.

This experienced social services manager will listen to what everyone has to say, and will then reconsider the situation.

You will be told in writing what has been decided as soon as possible, and certainly within 28 days of your letter being received by us.

Step Three: You want a review

If your're not happy with this decision, you should tell the Designated Officer within 28 days.

The Designated Officer will arrange for a Review Panel to be brought together. This will be within 28 days of getting your letter. You will be invited to come along, and will be given at least ten days notice of the actual date.

The Review Panel will comprise two members of the County Council's Social Services Committee. The panel will be chaired by someone who is completely independent of both the County Council and any voluntary organisations which we deal with. The Designated Officer will be present to advise the Panel.

If you like you can bring someone with you for company or to speak on your behalf.

The Panel will review all the circumstances surrounding your complaint, and the investigation into it so far. It will recommend whatever action it considers appropriate.

This will be made known in writing to everyone involved as soon as possible after the hearing.

The recommendations of the Review Panel will be recorded and sent to the Director of Social Services. He will consider what action needs to be taken and tell everyone involved what he intends to do.

If you are still not happy with what has happened, you may contact the Local Government Ombudsman at 21 Queen Anne's Gate, London, SW1H 9BU. Tel: 071 222 5622.

Appendix 3: Statements of philosophy and policy for the provision of services — Norfolk Social Services

A Philosophical Basis for the Provision of Services

Whereas legislation gives to the Social Services Committee the residual responsibility to provide care, attention or control to people who are in need of them, it must be expected in any civilised community that citizens do have a responsibility to promote their own welfare and that of their family and fellow citizens. Much of the assistance of the Department will therefore be in partnership with individuals and their families.

Morever, it should be expected that the general services offered by other agencies should be flexible enough to cater for people who have problems in receiving the basic or usual service. In other words, it is wrong for the Social Services Department itself to set up alternative long-term educational, recreational, youth or housing facilities; we should be discussing with our colleagues in other agencies how handicapped and deprived people can make use of their facilities, rather than our acquiescing in social apartheid and making parallel provision.

Apart from statutory obligations to protect children and people who may have a psychiatric illness, the Department accepts that adult citizens in this Country have a right to reject offers of assistance, even if this means the continuance of a lifestyle which is disturbing to fellow citizens.

It also means that if we are to encourage independence and freedom in our clients, they will be exposed to the same physical and emotional risks as other members of society. We cannot protect people from every risk; one of the arts of social work is to achieve a balance between enabling a person to actualise their full potential and exposing them to undue risk. Whatever we do should be credible and defendable; decisions not to intervene need to be taken as carefully as those to take action.

B Policies and Action to put this Philosophy into effect

1. Services will be provided both equally and impartially to every resident of Norfolk no matter where they live in the County, in accordance with the decisions of the Social Services Committee and within the remit of the Local Authority Social Services Act, 1970. The following main tasks will be carried out:-

1.1 To investigate allegations that any child or adult is in need of care and attention not otherwise available to them, and where necessary, to provide services designed to protect them.

1.2 To arrange accommodation with families or in residential Homes, when it is no longer possible or appropriate to care for a person in his/her own home.

1.3 To work with an individual and his/her family to enable him/her, whenever possible, to live independently without further intervention by the Department.

1.4 To provide non-medical services which will enable patients to be discharged speedily from hospital into a supportive environment with adequate provision of Community Services, when they no longer require the medical and nursing care which can only be provided by residence in hospital.

1.5 To assess whether it is necessary for a person to be admitted compulsorily to hospital for phychiatric assessment and treatment, and if necessary to make the appropriate arrangements.

1.6 To give advice and assistance to families to promote the welfare of children and to prevent individuals from becoming in need of care and attention.

1.7 To contribute to the identification and alleviation or circumstances in the community which are likely to generate social stress.

2. When a person, however, cannot be supported adequately without the intervention of the Social Services Department, then we should take speedy and effective measures:-

2.1 To protect the individual.
2.2 To make a professional assessment of needs and of the resources which might be available to help.
2.3 To offer that amount of advice or care necessary to help a person tackle his/her problem.
2.4 To assist in a speedy return to independence with a consequent withdrawal of assistance.

3. Families who agree to cope with dependent relatives should have the opportunity of relieving themselves of the full burden by a flexible use of the Home Help Service, day care, voluntary Crossroads Schemes and short-term care. When developing networks of social care, the Department accepts that no one should live in a hospital unless they require the nursing and medical services which can only be provided by being resident in a hospital.

4. Residential care should only be offered if a person cannot be supported or protected in his/her own home or in a substitute one. There is an onus on the social worker, in partnership with the person's family, to have explored what support networks are available or could reasonably be developed before deciding on a residential placement.

5. Any person admitted to the residential care of the Department should be provided with as normal a life as possible. They should be treated as an individual, and any arrangements should allow for dignity and privacy. They should be allowed the maximum independence consonant with their welfare, and the maximum freedom of choice consonant with the orderly running of the residence and its other occupants. They should only be offered the care necessary to help them function independently, and should be encouraged to do for themselves any task which they are capable of doing. Both the person and his/her family should be involved in planning for the future. Residential care staff must know the purpose of a placement, and should work positively to achieve the objectives which have been set.

Services for Children and Families

Introduction

The experience of family life and growing up is many and varied both in terms of cultural norms and expectations, economic circumstances and quality of care. It is rarely smooth and has almost inevitable periods of trauma, crisis and breakdown. However, in the main, children and young people, even when their behaviour is of concern at some stage in their lives, mature successfully without the intervention of Welfare Agencies. For many, family life is rewarding, for most it is tolerable, but for a small number it can be destructive. The task facing the Social Services Department in fulfilling both its statutory and discretionary responsibilities is to ensure that it does not over-react to the 'normal' stresses and strains experienced by people whilst at the same time ensuring that it responds effectively and decisively when the need arises.

The Philosophical Basis

1. The best interests of the child should at all times be paramount.
2. Children should have a right to a scure and permanent relationshp with a familiar group of adults.
3. Children and families should share in the decisions determining their future.
4. Effective services for children and families can only be provided by the community at large and all appropriate agencies acting together.
5. The involvement of children and young people in the criminal justice system should be kept to a minimum.

Policies and Practices

1. *The best interests of the child should at all times be paramount.*

1.1 Any work underaken by the Department in situations where children are involved should be guided by this principle. It should override the interests, needs and desires of others.

1.2 When children are thought to be subject to threat or danger, the Department should act decisively in concert with other organisations to investigate and, if necessary, ensure their protection.

1.3 The Department should plan its intervention with children and families effectively to these ends. Its decision and actions should be subject to review and regular monitoring. The Department should act corporately, recognising that if the best interests of the child are to be fulfilled, the skills, expertise, knowledge and resources within it as a whole will be required. Consequently, key decisions should be shared and open to systematic scrutiny.

2. *Children should have a right to a secure and permanent relationship with a familiar group of adults.*

2.1 The Department should normally try to maintain children with their natural family and in their local area through the provision of complementary and supplementary services (e.g. childminding, playgroups, nurseries, Intermediate Treatment, social work support, counselling).

2.2 If the family network no longer exists or because it can no longer carry out its responsibilities in full or in part, the Department may need to consider substitute services. However, before this is undertaken it should explore the full resources of the child's network and community and should not assume that temporary or permanent incapacity to care for a child leaves no alternative to the department taking over parenting.

2.3 The Department should attempt to keep parents and children together physically and emotionally by:-

(i) taking determined action to prevent reception into care,

(ii) minimising children's emotional separation from families whilst in care by facilitating access arrangements and encouraging and enabling contact.

(iii) implementing vigorous plans for the rehabilitation of children back to their own families and communities.

2.4 When it is necessary for the Department to substitute the parenting of the natural family, its actions should be decisive and alternative arrangements made with urgency. A plan which is designed to either return the child to the natural family or into independent living within a given time span, or, to secure permanent substitute care, should be drawn up by the Department and acted upon.

2.5 In making arrangements for substitute care the Department should presume in favour of a family placement in the local area and ensure that such possibilities are available.

2.6 Residential care has a positive place in the total pattern of services available to families and children. However, under normal circumstances a residential placement would not be appropriate unless it is able to offer something positive that other placements cannot.

2.7 Placement of children in residential care should not entail any undue diminution of the rights and personal independence of actions that they would normally have.

2.8 Children in the care of the Department should only be restrained if they are a proven danger to themselves or others.

2.9 When children leaving care are unable to return to their families, the Department should prepare them for independent living through social skills training, the provision of supported accommodation and adequate after care.

3. *Children and families should share in the decisions determining their future.*

3.1 It is important that children and families should be in a position to question professional attitudes and challenge the exercise of power that the Department has.

3.2 Children and families should, wherever possible and according to their age and understanding, have access to information about themselves, be informed about what might happen to them and to be actively involved in the decision making process through attendance at case conferences and reviews. Work undertaken by the Department with children and families should, wherever feasible, be undertaken on a contract basis which is understandable and acceptable to all concerned.

3.3 Reports to the Courts and other tribunals about children and families should be open to them according to the limits that the law allows and depending on the confidentiality of the information involved.

3.4 The Department should only seek to take on parental rights in full or part when other methods have failed and children and families should always be advised and helped to seek legal advice in all situations when their rights could be threatened.

4. *Effective service for children and families can only be provided by the community at large and all appropriate agencies acting together.*

4.1 Children and families often require the services of the Department through reasons of poverty, inadequate housing, poor education, lack of 'natural' support and the inability to avail themselves of the resources necessary to maintain a fulfilled existence. The Department cannot tackle these problems or the actions and behaviour that may result from them alone, but must work in concert with the local community, voluntary organisations, other local authority departments, the Health Service, DHSS and those agencies associated with the juvenile justice system.

4.2 The Department should encourage and support the ability of family networks and local committees to care for those children and families who are in need.

4.3 The Department should encourage and support people from the local community to provide specific services, such as befriending and fostering, for children who might otherwise have to leave that community.

4.4 The Department should act as an enabler, helping children and families in need to make better use of generally available services and to advise them of their rights to these services. The Department should not normally provide services that it is the responsibility of other organisations to deliver.

4.5 When it is necessary for the Department to provide a special service for a child, such as education, every effort should be made to reintegrate that child into the generally available service in a planned manner and at the earliest opportunity.

5. *The involvement of children and young people in the criminal justice system should be kept to a minimum.*

5.1 In concert with other organisations the Department should develop ways of preventing crime through situational and social measures.

5.2 Given the fact that juveniles who become involved in formal judicial proceedings are more likely to reoffend than those who do not, the Department should actively encourage efforts to divert offenders from Court through the Police Cautioning system.

5.3 Given the dangers of "tariff acceleration" interventions by the Department and, in particular, recommendations in Social Enquiry Reports, should be carefully considered before submission to Court.

5.4 Given the failure of Detention Centres and Youth Custody to benefit children in any positive manner, recommendations in Social Enquiry Reports for such penal establishments should never be made unless the public cannot be protected in any other way.

5.5 If children need to be in the care of the local authority such an order should be sought through care proceedings rather than through criminal proceedings.

Services for Disabled People

Disabled people do not constitute an homogenous group. People of all ages, personalities and backgrounds are variously affected by a wide range of conditions. Consequently, attitudes to disablement and aspirations to independence are equally as varied amongst disabled people and their carers as amongst the public at large. Recent years have, however, generally seen a growing awareness and acceptance of disability and an increasing acknowledgement of the "normal" needs and potential of disabled people.

Using the Chronically Sick and Disabled Persons Act, 1970, as a basis, Social Services provision seeks to encourage this trend both for individuals and for disabled people in general. It seeks to provide both a sensitive approach response to the personal needs of individuals and those caring for them, with an active contribution to reducing the physical limitations which exist within the Community.

The Philosophical Basis of Social Services Provision

1. The Social Services Department should improve society's awareness of its responsibility to provide for and accept the handicaps of disabled people.
2. Intervention, care and support should be determined in conjunction with the individual and his family as a result of a professional assessment of their need.
3. *Services should aim at integration in the community's activities rather than reliance upon segregation or specialised provision.*
4. Services and resources should be multi-disciplinary and be available to the client in his/her own locality.
5. Help should offer the maximum provision of choice for the individual and the minimal loss of independence and control over his/her life.

Policies and Practices

1. *To improve society's awareness of its responsibilities to provide for and accept the handicaps of disabled people.*

1.1 Work with architects, planners, public agencies and services, commercial enterprise and institutions to ensure that the general environment of buildings and public and commercial facilities are not restricted by virtue of their design and construction to non-handicapped people.

1.2 Work with self-help, voluntary and community groups to provide resources that can be used by disabled people and those who assist in their caring.

1.3 The promotion amongst *the public* and other agencies of the knowledge that handicapped people have the same needs as non-handicapped people, but that realising and satisfying them is often more difficult.

1.4 Promote the availability of service and resource information.

2. *Intervention, care and support should be determined in conjunction with the individual and his/her family as a result of a professional assessment of their need.*

2.1 Social Services personnel should be skilled in the assessment of individual needs, and have professional experience and understanding of the particular needs and problems of these clients. This would include some knowledge of the physically handicapping disease or traumatic processes and their treatment options.

2.2 Social Services personnel should be knowledgeable of the psychological and social effects of the disability upon other members of the family and be able to assist them accordingly.

2.3 Social Services personnel should have a sound working knowledge of the range of appropriate resources and welfare benefits.

2.4 Programmes of care should be based upon the principles of maximum individual choice and dignity and the retention of client control over their lives.

2.5 There should be an initial comprehensive professional assessment followed by regular reviews and evaluation directed towards the greatest possible degree of independence for the client.

3. *Services should aim at integration in the community's activities rather than reliance upon segregated or specialist provision*

3.1 Special provision of resources solely for disabled people should be avoided as far as possible unless there is a clear need and benefit to the individual or his/her family.

3.2 Social Services staff should be conversant with an imaginative in their use of local community facilities and be prepared to act as advocate for the inclusion and participation of clients in an ordinary range of activities or groups.

3.3 Where segregated facilities exist their objectives should include that of restoring the client to full community involvement and integration as far as it is possible to do so.

4. *Services and resources should be multi-disciplinary and as far as possible be available to the client in his/her own locality.*

4.1 There is a responsibility to ensure that co-ordination of service and treatment from other agencies in addition to Social Services takes place. This requirement can be critical for disabled clients.

5. *Help should offer the maximum provision of choice for the individual and the minimal loss of independence and control over his/her life.*

5.1 Wherever possible, resources should be provided to enable the individual to stay in his/her own home or to live in ordinary or adapted housing.

5.2 If a specific specialist provision of residential or day care resource is necessary, it should be actively provided. Social Services staff should always ensure that the highest degree of independence and choice is available commensurate with the client's needs and competence. It should not diminish their choice of their own life styles.

Services for Elderly People

Old age is not a problem in itself, but a period of life when environmental, physical and emotional problems are more likely to arise. The term 'elderly' encompasses a broad age range and includes fit, active and independent people as well as those who because of increasing frailty, illness or disability need practical and emotional support to maintain their lifestyle.

The Department's services are principally geared to this second group, but through its co-operation with other statutory agencies and voluntary organisations it contributes to provision for a wider group of elderly people who otherwise might not be clients of the Department.

Services are provided with the aim of enabling elderly people and their carers to live full and satisfying lives as close to what they regard as 'normal' as can be achieved within the limits imposed by their situation.

As an overall principle, help should not be imposed on any elderly person without consent except in those rare cases where the Mental Health Act 1983 or the National Assistance Act 1948 (Section 47) apply.

The Philosophical Basis of Social Services Provision

1. Help should be provided in such a way and to such an extent as to enable elderly people to remain in a home of their own as long as a quality of live can be maintained which is acceptable to them.

2. Where mental or physical capacity is limited, help should aim to assist those who can to overcome their difficulties and enable those who cannot to bear them with as little loss of activity or independence as possible.
3. Where it is not practicable or desirable for an elderly person to continue to live in a home of their own, alternatives such as living with relatives, sharing another home or moving into residential care should be explored.
4. Where residential care is appropriate the aim should be to achieve the best quality of life for each person, recognising that the interests of the individual resident and the resident group have to be balanced.
5. The needs of the elderly person's family or carers must be recognised and met.
6. Social Services Department help should be provided in co-operation with other Agencies both statutory and voluntary.

Policies and Practices

1. Help should be provided in such a way and to such an extent as to enable elderly people to remain in a home of their own as long as a quality of life can be maintained which is acceptable to them.

1.1 Definition of needs must not be based solely on the service available but on skilled multi-disciplinary assessment of the individual's quality of life and of the help needed to be able to maintain and improve it.

1.2 Services should be introduced sensitively and in response to an assessed need. It should be appreciated that whilst increased dependency attracts increasing care, increasing care risks increasing dependence.

1.3 The policy requires a priority to be given to the development and use of domiciliary services, day and relief care.

1.4 Education is required amongst staff of this and other agencies and the general public to recognise the anxieties provoked in relatives and neighbours by frail elderly people living alone and to encourage tolerance of the risks involved.

2. *Where mental or physical capacity is limited, help should aim to assist those who can to overcome their difficulties and enable those who cannot to bear with them with as little loss of activity or independence as possible.*

2.1 Limitations arising from mental or physical impairment should not be considered an inevitable part of the ageing process. Opportunities for active rehabilitation to maintain or regain daily living skills and to minimise the effects of disability should be encouraged.

2.2 Aids and adaptions should be provided to assist in this process.

3. *Where it is not practicable or desirable for an elderly person to continue to live in a home of their own, alternatives such as living with relatives, sharing another home or moving to residential care should be explored.*
3.1 Considerations of alternatives to living at home should be undertaken in conjunction with the client and his family and with due regard to the emotional implications of such a major decision.
3.2 Careful preparation for such a move should take place carefully and at a pace the client can tolerate. Where the move is not within his/her family, opportunities for introductions and final stays should be provided
3.3 Elderly people and their relatives should not be led to believe that admission to residential care is necessarily final and they should be encouraged to feel able to determine their own lifestyle within residential care.
3.4 Where it is accepted that the elderly person's need for residential care is indefinite, a further move should only take place as the result of a careful reassessment in which the resident takes a full part.

4. *Where residential care is appropriate the aim should be to achieve the best quality of life for each person, recognising that the interests of the individual resident and the resident group have to be balanced.*
4.1 The way a residential home is run should be adapted as far as possible to meet the needs of the individual resident rather than expecting the latter to conform to a fixed routine.
4.2 The right to privacy and opportunities to exercise personal choice should be extended to all residents.
4.3 The Department should exercise its registration and inspection responsibilities under the Registered Homes Act 1984 in a way that encourages the provision of a high quality of care.
4.4 In enforcing the standards described in "A Home Life", the Department should seek an evenhandedness between standards expected in Private, Voluntary and Local Authority Homes.

5. *The needs of the elderly person's family or carers must be recognised and met.*
5.1 This policy requires the establishment of a system of "caring for the carers", if appropriate services should be provided notwithstanding the presence in the household of an able-bodied person.
5.2 Support to carers either as individuals or in groups should be developed and consideration given to the information needs of carers.
5.3 In responding to the assessed needs of elderly people, the often considerable needs of their carers must be borne in mind and services provided with due regard to the needs of both.

6. *Social Services Department help should be provided in co-operation with other agencies, both statutory and voluntary.*
6.1 Services should be jointly planned in accordance with mutually agreed philosophies and policies.
6.2 The provision of help to elderly people should be assessed and coordinated by the agencies in collaboration.
6.3 The Department should undertake to support the development of voluntary initiatives and monitor their progress providing where necessary training and financial advice.

Services for People with Mental Handicaps

Of all client groups, people with mental handicaps have traditionally experienced both the public's and professionals' emphasis on their disabilities rather than on their shared humanity. Intellectual impairment has been the reason for segregated provision of care and diminished opportunities in every sphere of life. This is now generally recognised to be an injustice of tragic proportions; changes in attitudes and practices now aim to a full recognition of the personal worth of the individual within the total society of which he/she is a part and his/her right to participate as fully as possible in all aspects of that society.

1. *The philosophical basis of social services provision*
Services shall be built upon the following principles:
1.1 The statement from the United Nations Declaration on the Rights of People with Mental Handicaps.
1.2 The principle of normalisation which asserts that services for individuals with special needs should be services which are valued in other parts of our society.
1.3 The concepts incorporated in the Jay report of normal patterns of life, preservation of individuality and personal planning.

2. The integration of the above principles will produce the following criteria for policy:
2.1 *Mentally handicapped people should have the right to normal patterns of life within the community.*
2.1.1 Mentally handicapped persons should enjoy as full a range of life opportunities and choices as their families, friends and the community can provide.
2.1.2 They should be enabled to become respected members of their communities and should not be devalued because of their intellectual impairment.

2.1.3 They should enjoy equal rights of access to normal services and be obliged to rely on special services only where they have a special need which cannot be met by services available to the general public.

2.1.4 This principle also means that help in making opportunities and providing the kind of choices that make for a full life is not solely the concern and responsibility of professionals, whether they are working for statutory or voluntary bodies, but is rather one for the society as a whole.

2.1.5 Positive encouragement is needed for all those who have the good will and the concern to help mentally handicapped people to open out their lives. The role of professionals should be to guide, to counsel and to encourage as well as to provide direct services.

2.1.6 Social Services personnel should be knowledgeable of the psychological and social effects of the disability upon other members of the family and be able to assist them accordingly.

2.2 *Mentally handicapped people should have the right to be treated as individuals*

2.2.1 It is not enough to provide services and to promote the integration of mentally handicapped people in their communities unless these efforts help to develop independence and self-fulfilment. No universally applicable formula or pattern of service can be prescribed for all the needs of mentally handicapped people. Each has different needs, capabilities and aspirations which need to be identified and which must guide the efforts of service providers.

2.2.2 This principle also means that mentally handicapped people and their families must play a full part in decisions which are intended to help them.

2.2.3 Alongside the recognition that care must be primarily a means of stimulating development and widening opportunities for a fuller life, necessarily goes the acknowledgement that it must also involve a degree of adventure. Service providers will need the active guidance and support of the employing authority in an approach to the needs of mentally handicapped people which emphasises development and quality of life and will enable them to encounter ordinary hazards of life without being over-protected. The community at large will also have an important part to play in this.

3. *Mentally handicapped people require additional help from the communities in which they live and from professional services if they are to develop their maximum potential as individuals.*

This does not mean substituting professional or outside lay judgements for those of mentally handicapped people and their families. But it does mean developing contacts and informing choices. The importance of supporting the caring efforts of the families of mentally handicapped people cannot be over-emphasised. Perhaps the greatest challenge is to provide support services which will relieve the hardships for families who continue to care for mentally handicapped people, and those which enable mentally handicapped people to live as independently as possible when they wish to leave home or when their families are no longer able to care for them.

3. *Objectives of Service Provision and Practice*
These imply the development of a comprehensive pattern of integrated local services and provision of support so that:

3.1 People with mental handicaps can live in their own homes as far as is possible; an imaginative range of support services should be provided to enable them to do so.

3.2 A variety of residential resources are available to meet the individual needs of children and adults on a non-institutionalised basis.

3.3 Provision is made for purposeful work and leisure using integrated rather than segregated facilities wherever possible.

3.4 All people with mental handicaps will have an individual plan based on the assessment of individual people's strengths and needs. It will be subject to regular reviews and will include the acquisition of skills, opportunities for experience, resources and services. The client's views will also be incorporated with the aim of understanding and furthering his/her emotional needs.

3.5 Services for mentally handicapped children will be provided in accordance with practice applied to those for children in care.

Services for People with Mental Health Problems

What constitutes being 'mentally ill' is an area of considerable public as well as philosophical, clinical and psychological debate. It can be described as an exaggerated extension of normal behaviour and the problem of defining mental illness is related to where the boundary comes between normal and abnormal behaviour. The layman's stereotype of the 'mad' person exhibiting a range of bizarre and possibly violent symptoms represents only a small percentage of people who are suffering severe mental distress; a majority of people will experience at some time levels of anxiety or depression or confusion which impair personal and social functioning to a lesser or greater extent. Most will recover their equilibrium without further help but there will be some who will need support and treatment of different kinds from different agencies and for varying lengths of time. This document seeks to define the basis on which social service involvement in this process should be determined, bearing in mind that our task is to alleviate personal, family and social stresses aggravating the conditions.

The philosophical basis of social services provision

(i) There should be professional encouragement of society's responsibility towards those of its members who are mentally ill or suffering psychological distress.

(ii) The client should be valued as a full citizen with rights and responsibilities, entitled to be consulted and to have an active opportunity to shape and influence relevant services, no matter how severe his or her disability.

(iii) Help should be aimed at offering the maximum provision of choice for the individual and the minimum loss of independence and control over his/her own life with due regard to the rights and interests of others.

(iv) Services should aim at integration in the community's activities rather than segregated provision and the main emphasis should be on fostering and maintaining mental health rather than alleviating the effects of mental illness.

(v) Intervention, care and support should be individually determined, based on a professional assessment of need and carried out only with the full knowledge and consent of the client except where statutory compulsory action is involved.

(vi) Services and resources should as far as possible be available to the client in his own locality and built upon multi-disciplinary approaches to identified needs.

Policies and practices

1. *The professional encouragement of society's responsibility towards those of its members who are mentally ill or suffering psychological distress.*

1.1 Work with self-help, voluntary and community groups to provide resources that can be used by the mentally ill and those who care for them.

1.2 The development of knowledge and skills amongst the public at large in the field of mental health.

2. *Help should be aimed at offering the maximum provision of choice for the individual and the minimum loss of independence and control over his own life.*

2.1 A range of residential and day care services should be developed and organised so that individual clients can enjoy the highest degree of independence possible commensurate with their needs and competence.

2.2 As far as possible there should be a range of accommodation, day care and activities which can meet the needs of clients but also allow them to make choices themselves in their own preferred life-styles.

3. *Services should aim at integration in the community's activities rather than segregated provision.*

3.1 In the provision of resources separate arrangements for the mentally ill should be avoided as far as posible except where there is a clear benefit to be derived from so doing.

3.2 Social Workers and allied professionals should be conversant with and imaginative in their use of local community facilities and prepared to act as advocate for the inclusion of individual clients in a variety of activities or groups.

3.3 Where segregated facilities exist they should be encouraged to retain as an objective the ultimate restoration of the client to full community involvement.

4. *Intervention, care and support shall be individually determined and based on professional assessment of need*

4.1 Statutory duties and responsibilities under the MHA concerning compulsory admission, consideration of alternative facilities for care and treatment and the provision of after care must, by law, be undertaken by approved Social Workers who have been given appropriate training to undertake the assessment process for approval and have reached satisfactory levels of professional competence to undertake these tasks.

4.2 Social service personnel should be skilled in the assessment of individual and family needs and have professional experience and understanding of the particular needs and problems of this client group.

4.3 Programmes of care should be based on the principles of the maximisation of individual choice and dignity and the retention of client control over their lives.

4.4 Continuing support should be subject to regular evaluation and should be directed towards ultimate independence of the client.

5. *Services and resources shall as far as possible be available to the client in his own locality and built upon multi-disciplinary approaches.*

5.1 There is a responsibility to ensure that links are made and there is access to other professionals and resources who are part of the assessment and care programme.

5.2 Whilst services should be accessible to the individual client, it should also be remembered that on occasion it is desirable to provide help away from the home base.

Day Care

Day care is a key part of the department's overall provision aimed at maintaining people in their own homes with independence and dignity. It may, but will not necessarily, take place in Centres. The concept of 'normalisation' requires seeking to ensure people are not prevented from gaining access to 'normal' community facilities because of age and disability. Day Care therefore seeks to complement and not replace normal provision. It has a maintenance role by offering care and attention which is not otherwise available, but in meeting social or physical needs it should aim also to develop or contribute to regaining confidence and skills which make possible access to wider local provision. The whole process requires a multi-disciplinary approach and commitment. Day Care needs to be local, accessible and available at the time required.

1. **The Philosophical Basis**
   1. Development of Day Care Services should be sufficiently flexible to meet the needs of the individual and his/her carers.
   2. Work with individual clients will be geared to providing care and attention which is not otherwise available to him/her and to helping him/her acquire or regain skills.
   3. The aim is to develop and maintain independence by allowing access to opportunities normally associated with daily life.
   4. Work should be undertaken with other Departments or Agencies to ensure that a range of provision is developed and in a way that means it is accessible to all members of the community.

2. **Policies and Practices**

   1. *Development of Day Care Services should be sufficiently flexible to meet the needs of the individual and his/her carers.*

   1.1 This demands the existence of a range of provision which may have a social, therapeutic or developmental base.

   1.2 Opportunities for day care need to be available near to the client avoiding lengthy journeys.

   1.3 Care should be available when required, including early mornings, evenings and weekends.

   2. *Work with individual clients will be geared to provide care and attention which is not otherwise available to him/her and to helping him/her acquire or gain skills.*

      2.1 Day Care needs to be available for people at a high degree of physical or emotional risk for whom carers are either not available or are in need of periods of relief.

2.2 A full assessment to include the needs of the client and associated carers must be undertaken.

2.3 A response to meet identified needs should be developed and plans made for ongoing review and re-assessment.

2.4 It must be recognised that the provision of any form of Day Care can be part of a combination of responses provided by the Department and other Agencies. As such it can only be successful if considered in relation to other components of the package. A key worker needs to be identified who will take responsibility for co-ordination, monitoring and review.

3. *The aim is to develop and maintain independence by allowing access to opportunities normally associated with daily life.*

3.1 This involves identifying activities with the client which are not or are no longer available to him/her due to physical, emotional or other functional limitations and to which he/she wishes to gain or regain access.

3.2 It demands identifying and/or creating opportunities to gain skills, knowledge and confidence which will allow that access.

3.3 For those clients whose need is for longer term care to develop and maintain motivation, to develop skills and confidence, or to relieve carers, a comprehensive range of opportunities throughout the day need to be available.

4. *Work should be undertaken with other Departments or Agencies to ensure that a range of provision is developed.*

4.1 This involves identifying gaps in both normal and special provision and making them known to organisations in the statutory and independent sectors.

4.2 It involves sharing experience and expertise with statutory Private and Voluntary organisations to develop new resources and effectively maintain existing ones.

4.3 Where new community facilities are being developed encouragement should be given to ensure they are accessible to all members of the community.